Christine McFadden is  r,
writing cookery books d
nutrition for various co g
a writer, she was a suc g
visual sense is carried through to her colourful recipes, as is
her love of lively ingredients.

Christine is an enthusiastic herb and vegetable gardener
and enjoys growing unusual plants. She lives in Bath with
her husband, Ed, and her cat, Maxwell.

HEALTHY MAIN MEAL SOUPS

CHRISTINE McFADDEN

Photographs by Don Last

LITTLE, BROWN AND COMPANY

BOSTON NEW YORK TORONTO LONDON

A LITTLE, BROWN BOOK

First published in the United Kingdom
by Little, Brown and Company (UK) in 1998

A CIP catalogue for this book is available
from the British Library

ISBN 0 316 88347 6

Typeset by Solidus (Bristol) Limited
Printed and bound in Great Britain by
Clays Ltd, St Ives plc

Little, Brown and Company (UK)
Brettenham House
Lancaster Place
London WC2E 7EN

Contents

Introduction

More and more people say they could live off soup, and indeed soup does seem to be the answer when you're too busy to cook, or don't know what to cook, or simply don't feel like eating very much. A well-prepared soup gives you a feeling of well-being which can help lift fatigue, is easy to digest but still satisfying, and is perfect for both solitary meals and for serving to crowds.

For many of us, the pressure and speed of life cuts down on the time we are able to spend on cooking, but we still want to eat healthily and well. Although a seemingly simple and health-promoting solution, soups are not always as nourishing as one would think. Main meal soups, however, are a different story. By using a wide range of fresh, appetising ingredients, you can produce satisfyingly hearty soups which provide the body with all the nutrients necessary for good health, without having to spend too long in the kitchen. Even the simplest of soups can be transformed into a main meal soup if you add interesting flavourings, pulses, grains, cheese, morsels of meat or fish, and serve it with tasty embellishments, good bread and perhaps a salad too.

Many of the classic main meal soups are what I call two-meal soups. The broth is strained and eaten separately, while the meat is sliced and served with vegetables, which are either cooked in the soup or freshly prepared. Delicious though they are, the preparation and serving of such soups requires time and devotion. To my mind, the best main meal soups are those that are simple to make and dish up, but are hearty enough to leave you feeling satisfied and well nourished. So although you'll find some traditional 'two-meal' classics in this book, the majority of recipes are simple, and some are even quick, to prepare. You'll find recipes here for thick, chunky one-pot meals, vibrantly coloured purées, spicy clear soups packed with noodles, vegetables and tasty pieces of poultry or fish, as well as ideas for exciting and quickly prepared accompaniments.

You'll also find recipes for a wide range of stocks which will make stock cubes a thing of the past.

WHAT MAKES A GOOD SOUP?

Almost anything can be turned into a soup, including left-overs. Tasty chunks of cooked fish, meat and poultry or cooked pulses and grains are all good candidates. That said, good quality left-overs make good quality soup, so don't throw in dubious items that have been lurking in the back of the fridge for a week. The choice of ingredients ulti-mately boils down to your mood at the time, and the ability to see whatever you have to hand in terms of a soup.

Appearance and texture are as important as flavour. Forget about puréed soups of indeterminate colour and think vibrant instead! If you fancy a puréed soup, finely chop the ingredients, purée about two-thirds and leave the rest whole to give the soup character and texture. Swirl in creams and sauces of contrasting colour and flavour, or top with crunchy croûtons or crushed dry-fried nuts or seeds. Try the Indian method of 'tempering', which is simply dribbling hot oil and dry-fried spices over the finished soup. If you're going for a chunky soup, make sure your chunks really are chunky.

The cooking liquid is important too. Most soups benefit from a home-made stock (not as daunting to make as you might think), although a good quality commercially made stock is fine in some cases. Some soups require nothing more than water, milk or yogurt, and lively seasonings.

The perfect soup has a bright fresh flavour and colour. It should be well seasoned but not over-salty, and not at all greasy. If your soup contains chunks, they should fit easily on to a spoon, and if it's a smooth soup it goes without saying that there should be no unintentional lumps.

The fun of making soups is that they are infinitely flexible and wonderfully good-tempered. Soups don't need endless watching over, they can be cooked at a time to suit you and reheated as necessary, and they'll keep for a few days in the fridge or a few months in the freezer.

GROUND RULES FOR MAKING SOUP

Although soup-making is simple, a few techniques are worth noting. First, slice vegetables thinly and evenly. This allows them to properly absorb oil or fat during the preliminary frying and to cook evenly and thoroughly. Secondly, heat the oil gently before adding vegetables. If the oil is too hot, it seals and fries the surface of the vegetables and prevents them absorbing liquids later. Thirdly, cook vegetables slowly with the lid on for about 10 minutes before you add any liquid. This part of the process is sometimes called 'sweating' and that is exactly what vegetables do. They release their juices, and these add an agreeably mellow flavour which is the basis of all good soups. After the initial sweating, the lid may be removed or placed askew.

NUTRIENTS IN SOUPS

Soup is a dilute form of food with a nutritional value in direct proportion to the amount of solids it contains. Being mostly liquid, soups can leave us feeling temporarily full but not necessarily well nourished.

For a soup to be truly nourishing it should contain a high proportion of solids and correspondingly less liquid. It becomes obvious that the line between a soup and a stew is a fine one – I think the bottom line is whether or not you need a spoon to eat it.

A nutritionally balanced soup should contain reasonable amounts of protein, carbohydrate, fibre, vitamins and minerals. If a soup is lacking in any of these, you can serve it with tasty embellishments and accompaniments to make up for any nutritional deficiencies. You'll find plenty of ideas for these in the Additions and Accompaniments chapter.

PLANT POWER

It is no accident that the longest chapters in this book are devoted to soups in which vegetables, grains and pulses form the major ingredients.

Nutrition is a constantly evolving science and fads seem to come and go overnight. However, scientists now seem to agree on what the early herbal healers already knew – that everyday plant foods such as carrots and cabbages are rich in pharmacological substances, known as phytochemicals, which range from anticoagulants and cholesterol reducers to immune system boosters and cancer blockers.

One of the fastest-growing areas of nutritional research is the study of antioxidants – a group of vitamins and minerals which protect the body's cells from oxidative damage by deactivating harmful molecules known as free radicals. By doing so, they reduce the risk of certain cancers and may help prevent heart disease.

The most common antioxidants are the carotenoids, vitamins C and E and the minerals selenium, zinc, manganese and copper. Carotenoids, which include beta- and alpha-carotenes, lycopene and lutein, are found mainly in orange- and red-fleshed fruit and vegetables, and also in dark green leafy vegetables.

It all seems to point to the same thing: people who eat large amounts of plant foods have a hugely reduced risk of cancer and heart disease compared with those who don't.

NUTRIENTS

The nutrients in food do not work in isolation, but form a tightly knit team which supplies the body's entire needs. It is helpful to have an understanding of their individual functions and to know the main food sources.

Protein

Proteins are vital for the growth, repair and maintenance of the body. They are made up of chains of amino acids, eight of which are essential since the body cannot make them for itself. Protein from plant foods is usually deficient in one or more of these amino acids. However, when plant foods from different sources are combined, the protein quality is improved. Good examples of protein combining are serving bread or tortillas with bean soups, or mixing beans and rice together in the same soup. Another tip is to swirl in cream or to include diced cheese in plant-based soups. If you are a vegetarian, it is particularly important to eat a wide range of grains, pulses, nuts and seeds in order to get adequate protein.

Good sources: Meat, poultry, fish, seafood, dairy products, eggs, tofu, grains, pulses, nuts.

Carbohydrate

The complex sugars, starches and cellulose (fibre) found in carbohydrate-rich foods are an important source of the fuel that produces the energy our bodies need, both to keep us going and for physical work and exercise. The other fuel sources are fat and, in certain circumstances, protein. Current nutritional guidelines recommend that we increase the amount of carbohydrate in the diet to supply 70 per cent of our energy needs. For most of us, this means doubling our intake.

Good sources: Root vegetables, grains, pulses, pasta, wholemeal bread.

Fat

Although you should be careful about the amount of fat you eat, it is an important part of a healthy diet. Fats and oils provide us with energy in a more concentrated form than carbohydrate. They also provide warmth, essential nutrients and improve the flavour and palatability of food. The World Health Organisation recommends that fat should provide no more than 30 per cent of our energy needs. Most of us in the UK eat almost three times this amount, so we all need to cut down.

Good sources: Meat, poultry, oily fish, dairy products, eggs, nuts, avocados.

Fibre

Dietary fibre is a form of carbohydrate (sometimes called non-starch polysaccharide) found in the structural material that makes up the roots, stems, leaves, seeds and fruits of plants. It reduces the risk of bowel cancer, heart disease, obesity and diabetes. It also stimulates the digestive system, helps prevent constipation, and makes us feel full, therefore potentially reducing calorie intake.

Good sources: Root vegetables, green vegetables, sea vegetables, fruit, grains, pulses, wholemeal pasta and bread.

Vitamin A

Vitamin A, also known as retinol, comes from animal sources, while carotenes are found in fruit and vegetables. The vitamin is essential for vision in dim light, and for the maintenance of healthy skin and mucus membranes.

Good sources: Dairy products, margarine, eggs, liver, oily fish.

Carotenes

Carotenes are a precursor of vitamin A, converting to vitamin A only when the body needs it. Carotenes are important antioxidants which are strongly believed to reduce the risk of some cancers.

Good sources: Orange- and red-fleshed vegetables and fruit, dark green leafy vegetables.

B Vitamins

The B vitamins are a group of almost a dozen substances including eight actual vitamins, folate (the collective name for a group of acids), and several vitamin-like compounds. They are vitally important for our health. B vitamins are involved mainly with the release of energy from food within the body. They are required for the functioning of the immune system, the digestive system, the heart and muscles, and for the production of new blood cells. Some of the B vitamins have antioxidant properties.

Good sources: Meat, poultry, eggs, fish, cheese, pulses, grains, wholemeal bread, nuts, seeds.

Vitamin C

Vitamin C is essential for good health. It assists with the absorption of iron from food, helps with the formation of bones, teeth and tissues, speeds the healing of wounds, helps keep the skin elastic, and improves resistance to infection. It is an important antioxidant, protecting the body against the harmful effects of free radicals and thus reducing the risk of cancer. Our bodies cannot make vitamin C so it has to come from food. It is a very unstable vitamin and is easily destroyed by heat and oxidation.

Good sources: Vegetables, particularly peppers, chillies and dark leafy greens, fresh fruit.

Vitamin D

We need vitamin D for strong, healthy bones and teeth, and to maintain adequate calcium levels in the blood. Without it, the body cannot absorb calcium. Vitamin D comes from two entirely different sources: it can be manufactured directly by the body when the skin is exposed to sunlight, or it can be supplied by food.

Good sources: Eggs, liver, dairy products, margarine, oily fish.

Vitamin E

Vitamin E is an important antioxidant and as such protects the cells from oxidative damage and the risk of cancer. It boosts the immune system, prevents muscle inflammation and may help treat arthritis and some skin conditions. Vitamin E is also involved in red blood cell formation.

Good sources: Wheatgerm, safflower and sunflower oils, nuts and nut oils, olive oil, seeds, eggs, margarine, avocados.

Calcium

In addition to strengthening the bones, calcium is essential for muscle contraction (including the heart muscle), nerve function, enzyme activity and for clotting of the blood. Too little calcium in the diet results in stunted growth and rickets in young children, and osteoporosis (loss of bone) in post-menopausal women.

Good sources: Dairy products, fish, nuts, green leafy vegetables, fruit.

Magnesium

Magnesium is an essential constituent of the body cells. It activates energy-releasing enzymes and is required for muscle and nerve function. Studies show low magnesium levels may be associated with increased risk of heart disease.

Good sources: Grains, pulses, nuts, vegetables, fruit.

Iron

Iron is involved in the production of red blood cells, the functioning of several enzymes and in transporting oxygen around the body. A deficiency results in anaemia, the symptoms of which include tiredness, breathlessness, pale skin and irritability. Vitamin C promotes the absorption of iron, whereas oxalic acid (in spinach) and phytic acid (in grains) inhibit it.

Good sources: Red meat, liver, eggs, oysters, dried apricots.

Zinc

One of the most versatile of minerals, zinc regulates the activities of hundreds of enzymes and is involved in the metabolism of proteins, carbohydrate, energy and genetic material within the cells. It is essential for growth, especially of the foetus during pregnancy, for the formation of bone tissue, the development of reproductive organs, the healing of wounds and for maintaining a healthy immune system. It is also thought to be helpful in preventing and shortening colds.

Good sources: Meat, poultry, liver, seafood, eggs, milk, nuts, pulses.

Potassium

Potassium is needed for the normal functioning of the nerves and muscles, including the heart muscle, and is involved in enzyme activity and protein metabolism. It works in a complementary way to sodium (salt) in the functioning of cells and in the concentration and balance of fluids within the cells. Most of us have too much sodium in our diet and too little potassium.

Good sources: Green vegetables, fruit, dairy products, grains, pulses.

Selenium

Selenium is a trace element present in the soil. Levels differ from country to country – in some areas they are worryingly low and dietary deficiencies have been recorded. Although needed in very small amounts, selenium is important. It works in conjunction with vitamin E as an antioxidant. As such, it protects our cells from oxidative damage, inhibiting cancer and reducing the risk of heart disease.

Good sources: Nuts (especially Brazil nuts), seeds, pulses, fish, meat, wholemeal bread.

FAHRENHEIT CONVERSION CHART

°C	gas	°F
110	¼	225
120	½	250
140	1	275
150	2	300
170	3	325
180	4	350
190	5	375
200	6	400
220	7	425
230	8	450
240	9	475

METRIC/IMPERIAL MEASUREMENTS

Some of the imperial measurements may seem overly precise, but that is because the metric measurements have been rounded up and those are the ones I would encourage you to use. For example, it is easy to measure 150 g on the scales but obviously hard to measure 5½ oz – which is the exact imperial equivalent. By the year 2000, imperial measurements will be a thing of the past.

Vegetable Soups

The sheer versatility and variety of vegetables makes them a fruitful basis for an infinite number of soups which even the most reluctant vegetable eater will down with relish. Vegetables not only offer an inspiring range of tastes, textures and colours, they are also a rich source of health-promoting vitamins and minerals.

This chapter includes earthy root vegetable soups, creamy corn chowders, vibrant green soups made with leafy vegetables, robust tomato-based soups, and many more. In most cases, only one or two vegetables are used so that the flavours remain distinct, but there are also soups in which several vegetables combine to produce a rich complex flavour.

Many of the recipes feature vegetables that are roasted or chargrilled rather than fried before being incorporated in the soup. This is a marvellous way of intensifying their flavour since all the blackened bits and sticky juices can go into the soup as well. Colourful Mediterranean-style vegetables – peppers, big juicy tomatoes, courgettes, aubergines, red onions – are particularly good candidates. Roasting or grilling also helps cut down on fat since very little oil is needed, especially if you use a non-stick roasting tin or a ridged stove-top grill pan.

THE RECIPES

TUSCAN TOMATO AND BREAD SOUP

SERVES 4–6

Known in Italy as *pappa al pomodoro*, this thick soup makes a sustaining meal when served with plenty of Parmesan. Tomatoes are a rich source of vitamin C and lycopene, a carotene thought to help reduce the risk of some cancers.

300 g/11 oz stale unsliced farmhouse bread
4–5 tbsp olive oil
2 garlic cloves, finely chopped
2 tsp tomato purée
750 g/1 lb 10 oz large ripe tomatoes, peeled, deseeded and diced
1 litre/1³/₄ pints Chicken Stock (page 188)
salt and freshly ground black pepper
8–10 basil leaves, coarsely shredded
freshly grated Parmesan cheese, to serve

Preheat the oven to 180°C (170°C fan oven)/gas 4. Slice the bread thickly and remove the crusts. Toast in the oven for 6–8 minutes until dry but not browned. Break into small pieces.

Heat 3 tablespoons of the oil in a large frying pan and fry the garlic for about a minute until just golden. Stir in the tomato purée and the tomatoes. Bring to the boil then simmer over low heat for 5 minutes, stirring occasionally with a wooden spoon to break up the tomatoes.

Bring the stock to the boil in another large saucepan. Stir in the tomato mixture and the toasted bread. Season generously, then stir in the basil. Simmer over medium heat for 2–3 minutes. Remove the pan from the heat and leave to stand, uncovered, for about an hour.

When ready to serve, reheat and stir thoroughly. Pour into bowls and drizzle a little of the remaining olive oil over each. Serve with a bowl of freshly grated Parmesan.

GRILLED SWEETCORN AND CHILLI CHOWDER

SERVES 6

Made with freshly picked sweetcorn, this soup is out of this world. It's pretty good with shop-bought sweetcorn too. Look for ears with the husk completely covering the kernels – this helps prevent moisture loss. The kernels themselves should look plump and spurt a little liquid when pierced with your fingernail. Serve with warm Chilli and Coriander Corn Muffins (page 210) and some crumbly white cheese.

6 sweetcorn ears, husks removed
1 green pepper, halved and deseeded
1 fleshy red or green chilli
600 ml/1 pint semi-skimmed milk
1 tbsp sunflower or grapeseed oil
1 onion, finely diced
2–3 thyme sprigs
1 fresh bay leaf
2 potatoes, finely diced
600 ml/1 pint Chicken Stock (page 188) or
Light Vegetable Stock (page 181)
salt and freshly ground black pepper
chopped fresh coriander, to garnish

Place the corn and the green pepper halves, cut side down, in a grill pan under a very hot grill. Grill for 5 minutes, turning the corn occasionally. Add the chilli and grill with the corn and pepper for another 10 minutes, turning the corn and chilli occasionally. Remove and allow to cool.

When cool enough to handle, remove the kernels from the cobs with a sharp knife. Peel the pepper and chilli, remove the seeds from the chilli, and chop the flesh of both into small dice.

Purée half the corn with the milk in a food processor or blender until reasonably smooth.

Heat the oil in a saucepan and gently fry the onion with the herbs until the onion is translucent. Add the green pepper, chilli, potatoes, puréed corn and stock. Bring to the boil then simmer gently for 15 minutes. Add the remaining corn kernels and simmer for another 5 minutes.

Fish out the herbs and season the soup. For a smoother soup, purée half the mixture, then return this to the soup in the pan and reheat gently. Pour the soup into serving bowls and garnish with coriander.

AVOCADO, GREEN PEPPER AND CORIANDER SOUP

SERVES 4–6

This soup is ideal for a summer lunch. It is very rich so portions need not be gargantuan. I like to serve it at room temperature rather than chilled, so that the flavours are not muted. Serve with warm tortillas, Black Bean Salsa (page 228) and either crème fraîche or Roasted Pepper Cream (page 225) – or both!

1 green pepper, deseeded and roughly chopped
1 fresh green chilli, deseeded and roughly chopped
3 tomatoes, peeled, deseeded and roughly chopped
4 spring onions, green parts included, roughly chopped
425 ml/³/₄ pint Chicken Stock (page 188) or
Light Vegetable Stock (page 181)
3 large ripe avocados, halved and peeled
juice of 1¹/₂–2 limes
4 tbsp roughly chopped fresh coriander
¹/₂ tsp ground cumin
1 tsp sea salt
freshly ground black pepper

TO GARNISH
lime slices
fresh coriander sprigs

Put the green pepper, chilli, two of the tomatoes and the spring onions in a blender with 300 ml/¹/₂ pint of the stock. Blend for 2 minutes, then strain through a fine-meshed sieve, pressing well to extract all the juices.

Return the strained liquid to the blender with 2¹/₂ roughly chopped avocados, the juice of 1¹/₂ limes, the coriander, cumin, salt and some freshly ground pepper. Purée again and check the seasoning, adding a little more lime juice if necessary. Thin with the rest of the stock if you feel the soup is too thick.

Pour into individual bowls and garnish with a lime slice and a sprig of coriander. Dice the remaining piece of avocado and the tomato and serve in a small bowl alongside, with the other accompaniments.

ROASTED AUBERGINE AND PEANUT SOUP WITH ROASTED PEPPER CREAM

SERVES 4

Roasting aubergines is a good way to cook them without using an enormous amount of oil. If you use a non-stick roasting tin you will need hardly any. This is a lightish soup but you could make it more robust by adding some Lebanese Lamb Balls (page 223). Precook them and then reheat in the soup after you have puréed it.

3 small aubergines, cut crossways into 1 cm / $^1/_2$ inch slices
olive oil, for brushing
1 red onion, sliced into 1 cm / $^1/_2$ inch thick rings
2 garlic cloves, unpeeled
50 g / 1$^3/_4$ oz unsalted peanuts, dry-fried
1 litre / 1$^3/_4$ pints Chicken Stock (page 188) or
Vegetable Stock (page 180)
4–5 thyme sprigs
salt and freshly ground black pepper
Roasted Pepper Cream (page 225), made without chilli
chopped fresh coriander or
Sizzled Herbs (page 235), to garnish

Preheat the oven to 220°C (210°C fan oven)/gas 7. Lightly brush the aubergine slices with olive oil. Insert 3 wooden cocktail sticks into each onion ring from the outside edge to the middle, then brush the onion with oil too.

Place the aubergine, onion and garlic in a single layer in a non-stick roasting tin or baking tray, and roast in the pre-heated oven for 10 minutes. Remove the garlic and reserve, then continue to roast the aubergines and onion for another

15–20 minutes, turning occasionally, until the aubergines are browning nicely and the onion rings are beginning to blacken round the edges. Remove the cocktail sticks from the onions. Roughly chop the aubergines and onion rings. Peel the garlic and roughly chop that as well.

Put the peanuts in a blender and grind to a paste.

Put the vegetables and stock in a saucepan with the thyme and the peanut paste, and bring to the boil. Season, then cover and simmer for 10 minutes.

Fish out the thyme, then pour the mixture into a blender and process to a purée. Check the seasoning and reheat gently. Pour into bowls and swirl in some roasted pepper cream and a sprinkling of chopped fresh coriander or sizzled herbs.

ROASTED AUBERGINE, RED PEPPER AND CHILLI SOUP

SERVES 4–5

Roasted aubergines and peppers make a richly flavoured soup thickened with a fragrant mix of dry-fried ground seeds and oregano. Serve with Grilled Corn, Avocado and Tomato Salsa (page 228) and warm tortillas or pitta bread.

2 aubergines, cut crossways into 1 cm/^{1}/$_2$ inch slices
olive oil
1 red onion, sliced into 1 cm/^{1}/$_2$ inch thick rings
2 red peppers
2 fleshy red chillies
3 large garlic cloves, unpeeled
^{1}/$_2$ tsp cumin seeds
1 tsp coriander seeds
1 tbsp sesame seeds
1 tsp dried oregano
1 litre/1^3/$_4$ pints Roasted Tomato Stock (page 184)
sea salt and freshly ground black pepper
soured cream or Coriander Cream (page 231), to serve
chopped fresh coriander or
flat-leafed parsley, to garnish

Preheat the oven to 230°C (220°C fan oven)/gas 8. Lightly brush the aubergine slices with olive oil and place in a single layer in a non-stick roasting tin. Insert three wooden cocktail sticks into the onion slices from the outside edge to the middle, to hold the rings in place. Brush with oil and place in the tin with the aubergines. Put the peppers, chillies and garlic in the tin too – use two tins if necessary. Roast in the preheated oven, turning occasionally, until beginning to blacken (the chillies and garlic will need less time: remove them after about 10 minutes).

Meanwhile, put all the seeds in a small heavy-based frying pan without any oil. Dry-fry over medium heat for a minute or two until the seeds smell fragrant. Add the oregano and fry for a few seconds more – don't let the seeds or herb burn. Immediately remove from the heat and tip the mixture on to a plate to cool. Grind to a coarse powder with a pestle and mortar or in a blender.

Remove the cocktail sticks from the onion rings, the skin from the garlic and the skin and seeds from the chillies. Working over a bowl to catch the juices, remove the skin and seeds from the peppers.

Put all the vegetables into a food processor or blender with the ground seed mixture. Process to a purée, thinning with some of the stock. Pour the mixture into a saucepan together with the remaining stock. Bring to the boil, season, then simmer for 5 minutes.

Pour into bowls, swirl in the soured cream or coriander cream and sprinkle with coriander or parsley.

PARSNIP, SQUASH AND SWEET POTATO SOUP WITH GINGER AND CHILLI

SERVES 6

Sweet earthy root vegetables mellow the heat of ginger and chilli in this hearty autumnal soup. It's a good source of slow-release carbohydrate which will keep your energy levels up.

50 g/1¹/₂ oz butter or 2 tbsp sunflower oil
2.5 cm/1 inch piece fresh ginger root, finely chopped
1 fresh bay leaf
1 rosemary sprig
¹/₄–¹/₂ tsp dried chilli flakes
6 small parsnips, diced
1 butternut squash, prepared as described on page 14 then diced
1 sweet potato, diced
2 red onions, chopped
2 tbsp tomato purée
1 litre/1³/₄ pints Chicken Stock (page 188) or Vegetable Stock (page 180)
1 tsp salt
freshly ground black pepper
Greek yogurt or crème fraîche, to serve
Sizzled Sage (page 235) or chopped fresh coriander, parsley or chives, to garnish

Heat the butter or oil in a heavy-based saucepan. Add the ginger, bay leaf, rosemary and chilli flakes, and stir for a few seconds over medium heat to give the oil a bit of flavour.

Next add the vegetables, cover and let them sweat over medium-low heat for about 10 minutes. Stir in the tomato purée, cover and cook for a few minutes more.

Pour in the stock and season with the salt and some freshly ground pepper. Bring to the boil, then reduce the heat and simmer for 15–20 minutes until the vegetables are tender.

Fish out the bay leaf and rosemary. Purée about two-thirds of the soup in a food processor or blender. Return this to the soup in the pan, reheat gently and check the seasoning. Pour into shallow bowls, swirl in a spoonful of yogurt or cream and sprinkle with sizzled sage or chopped fresh herbs.

ROASTED SQUASH, CHILLI AND PUMPKIN SEED SOUP

SERVES 4

The garnishes really bring this soup to life, adding texture, colour and complex flavours as well as valuable nutrients. Delicious, dark amber pumpkin seed oil is becoming more widely available in larger supermarkets. If you can't find any, use extra-virgin olive oil instead. Serve the soup with hunks of Italian bread.

2 butternut squash
olive oil
1 large baking potato
2 garlic cloves, unpeeled
1 fresh red chilli
700 ml/1¼ pints Chicken Stock (page 188)
salt and coarsely ground black pepper

TO GARNISH
3 tbsp pumpkin seeds, dry-fried
3 tomatoes, peeled, deseeded and diced
50 g/1¾ oz firm white cheese such as
Wensleydale or feta, crumbled
pumpkin seed oil

Preheat the oven to 200°C (190°C fan oven)/gas 6.

To prepare the squash, cut in half crossways at the point where the rounded part meets the neck. Cut the skin off each piece. Quarter the rounded part and scrape away the seeds and fibres. Cut the neck in half lengthways and then cut each piece crossways into three.

Place the squash pieces in a roasting tin and brush with oil. Bake in the preheated oven for 45 minutes, turning occasionally, until beginning to blacken round the edges. Bake the potato at the same time.

Put the garlic and chillies in a small roasting tin and place in the oven after the squash has been roasting for 30 minutes. Roast until the garlic is soft and the chillies are beginning to blacken and blister. Remove the skin from the garlic and the skin and seeds from the chillies.

Put two-thirds of the roasted squash in a food processor or blender. Peel the baked potato and add the flesh, along with the garlic, chillies and about 300 ml/½ pint of the stock, to the squash. Blend to a purée.

Scrape the purée into a saucepan, and stir in the rest of the stock. Chop the whole pieces of squash into bite-sized chunks and add them too. Season with salt and pepper and reheat gently.

Ladle into bowls, sprinkle with the garnishes and finish with a swirl of pumpkin seed oil.

ROASTED TOMATO, RED PEPPER AND RED ONION SOUP WITH AÏOLI AND SIZZLED SAGE

SERVES 6

This is one of my favourite soups. Don't discard the blackened bits of vegetable flesh from under the skins – they add a lovely smoky flavour. Serve the soup hot or chilled. If serving chilled, garnish with fresh basil rather than sizzled sage. Serve with Chick-Pea and Feta Salsa (page 229) and, for a real blow-out, Bruschetta (page 207), Grilled Polenta (page 212) or Catalan Tomato Bread (page 208).

2 red onions, sliced into 1 cm / ¹/₂ inch rings
olive oil
6 garlic cloves, unpeeled
1 kg/2 lb 4 oz ripe plum tomatoes, halved crossways
4 red peppers
500 ml/18 fl oz Chicken Stock (page 188) or
Vegetable Stock (page 180)
sea salt and freshly ground black pepper
2 tsp wine vinegar

TO GARNISH
Aïoli (page 230)
Sizzled Sage (page 235) or shredded basil

Preheat the oven to 230°C (220°C fan oven)/gas 8. Insert 3 wooden cocktail sticks into the onion slices from the outside to the centre, to keep the rings in place. Brush with oil and place in single layer in a large, non-stick roasting tin, along with the garlic. Put the tomatoes and peppers in separate roasting tins, and trickle olive oil over the tomatoes (though not the peppers). Roast in batches in the preheated oven, turning the onions and peppers until all the vegetables are slightly blackened. The garlic will need 10 minutes; the onions, tomatoes and peppers about 20 minutes.

When cool enough to handle, peel away the skins from the peppers and discard the seeds – hold them over a bowl while doing this to save the juices.

Press the tomatoes through a sieve, discarding the seeds and skin. Squeeze the flesh from the garlic cloves and discard the skin. Remove the cocktail sticks from the onions.

Put the onions, garlic and peppers in a food processor or blender with the sieved tomatoes, pepper juice, stock and salt and pepper. Blend until smooth then stir in the vinegar. If serving cold, transfer to a bowl and chill for at least 2 hours. If serving hot, reheat gently and check the seasoning.

Pour into serving bowls and add a blob of aïoli. Top with sizzled sage or shredded basil.

CHILLED TOMATO, CUCUMBER AND PITTA BREAD SOUP

SERVES 4

This is lovely on a sweltering day when you don't want
to eat too much. Even so, the soup is quite filling.
If you don't have any roasted tomato stock, use
600 ml/1 pint chicken stock mixed with
300 ml/$^{1}/_{2}$ pint passata (bottled sieved tomatoes).
Sumac is a coarse dark red powder used as a seasoning
in Iran and the Lebanon. It has a lovely sharp
lemony taste. Serve the soup with a selection of Middle
Eastern-style accompaniments such as cooked bulgar
wheat, couscous or chick-peas, some cubed feta cheese
and small bowls of olives and pickled chillies.

$^{1}/_{2}$ *red onion, thinly sliced*
700 g/1 lb 9 oz ripe tomatoes, peeled, seeded and chopped
1 garlic clove, very finely chopped
1 small ridge cucumber, quartered lengthways, cut into
1 cm/$^{1}/_{2}$ inch pieces
425 ml/$^{3}/_{4}$ pint Chicken Stock (page 188)
425 ml/$^{3}/_{4}$ pint Roasted Tomato Stock (page 184)
1 tbsp balsamic vinegar
salt and freshly ground black pepper
2 large pitta breads, opened out flat
2 tbsp extra-virgin olive oil
1 tsp sumac (optional)
3 tbsp chopped flat-leafed parsley

TO GARNISH
1 avocado, halved, peeled and diced
chopped flat-leafed parsley

Put the onion slices in a bowl. Cover with boiling water and leave to stand for 5 minutes. Drain and allow to cool, then chop roughly.

Put the onions in a large bowl with the remaining vegetables and the stock. Stir in the vinegar and season with salt and plenty of pepper. Cover and chill for several hours or overnight.

Open out the pitta breads and toast in a moderate oven for a few minutes until crisp. Break into bite-sized pieces and toss in the olive oil and sumac, if using. Place in the bottom of individual serving bowls.

Add the parsley to the soup, then ladle the soup into the bowls. Leave to stand for a few minutes to soften the bread. Garnish with a spoonful of diced avocado and a sprinkling of parsley just before serving.

ASPARAGUS GAZPACHO

SERVES 4

A Spanish-style soup slightly different from the better-known tomato-based gazpacho. Serve with Bruschetta (page 207) or good rustic bread.

500 g / 1 lb 2 oz asparagus
1 litre / 1³/₄ pints Light Vegetable Stock (page 181) or
Chicken Stock (page 188)
4 slices stale white bread, crusts removed
2 tbsp olive oil
1 tsp lemon juice
salt and freshly ground black pepper

TO GARNISH
chopped hard-boiled eggs
Serrano ham, cut into thin strips
chopped spring onions

Cut the tips from the asparagus. Break the tough ends off the stalks, then slice the stalks into chunks. Plunge the tips into boiling water for 2 minutes. Drain, and set aside.

Put the stalks in a large pan with the stock. Bring to the boil and simmer for 15 minutes, until very tender. Remove from the heat and add the bread to the pan. Leave to soak for 10 minutes until softened. Transfer to a blender and purée with the oil and lemon juice. Return the purée to the pan, season, then cover and chill thoroughly.

When ready to serve, check the seasoning and add more lemon juice if necessary. Ladle into individual bowls and garnish with the reserved asparagus tips. Hand round the eggs, ham and spring onions in separate bowls.

FENNEL AND TOMATO SOUP WITH CHICK-PEA AND FETA SALSA

SERVES 4

Fennel adds a mildly liquorice flavour, but you could replace it with celery if you prefer. Serve with the salsa, some pitta bread and a green salad for a satisfying meal.

2 tbsp olive oil or extra-virgin sunflower oil
2 tsp fresh thyme leaves
1 onion, finely chopped
2 fennel bulbs, quartered, cored and cut into
neat 1 cm/$^1/_2$ inch dice
3 garlic cloves, very finely chopped
450 g/1 lb ripe plum tomatoes, peeled, deseeded and diced
150 ml/$^1/_4$ pint tomato juice
425 ml/$^3/_4$ pint Chicken Stock (page 188) or
Vegetable Stock (page 180)
$^1/_2$ tsp sugar
$^1/_4$ tsp dried chilli flakes
salt and freshly ground black pepper
6 kalamata olives, pitted and cut into slivers
3 tbsp chopped flat-leafed parsley
Chick-Pea and Feta Salsa (page 229), to serve

Heat the oil with the thyme in a large heavy-based saucepan. Add the onion and fennel and gently fry for about 10 minutes until tender. Add the garlic and fry for another minute.

Stir in the tomatoes, tomato juice, the chicken or vegetable stock, sugar, chilli flakes, and salt and pepper. Cover and simmer for 20 minutes.

Add the olives and parsley, and check the seasoning. Pour into shallow bowls and add a spoonful or two of the salsa.

FRENCH ONION SOUP

SERVES 4

A French classic and a guaranteed filler. All that's needed
to go with it is a simple green salad of nutty Little Gem or
Butterhead lettuce with some chopped fresh herbs.
Onions are a useful source of vitamin B6, folate
and vitamin C.

3 tbsp olive oil
750 g /1 lb 10 oz onions, thinly sliced
1 tsp salt
$^1/_4$ tsp sugar
40 g/1$^1/_2$ oz flour
150 ml/$^1/_4$ pint dry white wine or dry vermouth
2 litres/3$^1/_2$ pints boiling Rich Meat Stock (page 190) or
Chicken Stock (page 188), or half stock and water
freshly ground black pepper
2 tbsp brandy
12 rounds of French bread, toasted in a warm oven until hard
150 g/5$^1/_2$ oz Gruyère or Emmenthal cheese, grated

Heat 2 tablespoons of the oil in a large heavy-based
saucepan. Add the onions, cover and cook over low heat for
15 minutes. Uncover the pan, raise the heat to medium and
stir in the salt and sugar. Cook for 30–40 minutes, stirring
regularly, until the onions are a rich brown.

Sprinkle in the flour and stir for a minute. Pour in the
wine or vermouth, stirring thoroughly, then gradually
pour in the boiling stock, stirring continuously to prevent
lumps forming. Add pepper to taste, then simmer partially
covered for 30–40 minutes, skimming occasionally. Check
the seasoning.

Preheat the oven to 170°C (160°C fan oven)/gas 3. Just
before serving, stir the brandy into the soup, and pour into

an ovenproof tureen. Float the bread on top of the soup and spread the grated cheese over it. Drizzle with the remaining tablespoon of oil. Bake in the preheated oven for 20 minutes. Serve immediately.

SPRING VEGETABLE SOUP WITH MINT

SERVES 4

Young, tender vegetables and home-made stock are essential for this flavourful health-promoting soup. It is packed with vitamins and minerals including carotenes, vitamins C and E, folate, magnesium and iron. Serve it with good crusty bread, a selection of raw crunchy spring vegetables such as radishes, baby carrots and spring onions, and some extra crème fraîche for dipping.

850 ml/1¹/₂ pints Chicken Stock (page 188) or
Light Vegetable Stock (page 181)
6–8 small new potatoes, unpeeled
1–2 large mint sprigs
225 g/8 oz shelled young broad beans
5 tbsp chopped fresh mint
4 spring onions, green parts included, chopped
225 g/8 oz shelled peas
Little Gem lettuces, quartered and cut into thin segments
sea salt flakes and freshly ground black pepper
squeeze of lemon juice

TO GARNISH
crème fraîche
chopped fresh mint

Bring the stock to the boil and add the potatoes and the mint sprigs. Simmer until the potatoes are tender then add half the broad beans and cook for another minute. Remove the mint sprigs.

Pour two-thirds of the mixture into a food processor or blender, add the chopped mint and blend to a chunky purée. Return this to the soup in the pan.

Bring back to the boil and add the spring onions, peas, lettuce and remaining broad beans. Season well with sea salt and pepper. Simmer for 2–3 minutes more until the vegetables are just cooked but still bright green. Add a squeeze of lemon juice to brighten the flavour.

Ladle into bowls and add a blob of crème fraîche and a sprinkling of mint.

SPRING VEGETABLE SOUP WITH LEAFY GREENS

SERVES 6

Guaranteed to banish winter ills, this startlingly green soup gives the system a real spring-clean. Leafy greens are positively overflowing with beta-carotene, lutein and vitamin C − antioxidants essential for good health and thought to have cancer-fighting properties. They are also a useful source of iron, zinc and folate. Serve the soup with Stuffed Eggs (page 214) or quartered hard-boiled eggs, chewy hunks of rye bread and perhaps some cooked rice.

2 tbsp olive oil
4 baby leeks, cut into 1 cm/¹/₂ inch slices
3 small carrots, thickly sliced
8 new potatoes, preferably Roseval, unpeeled, cut into small chunks
1 small kohlrabi, cut into 1 cm/¹/₂ inch dice
3 tbsp chopped flat-leafed parsley
600 g/1 lb 5 oz mixed leafy greens such as rocket, spinach, nettles, watercress and sorrel, stalks removed, leaves chopped
1.2 litres/2 pints hot Chicken Stock (page 188) or Light Vegetable Stock (page 181)
115 g/4 oz shelled peas
3 tbsp chopped fresh dill
sea salt flakes and freshly ground black pepper
soured cream, smetana or crème fraîche, to serve

Heat the oil in a large saucepan and gently fry the leeks, carrots, potatoes and kohlrabi for a few minutes, covered. Add the parsley and half the leafy greens, and cook for a few seconds. Stir in about 425 ml/³/₄ pint hot stock. Simmer over medium heat, covered, stirring frequently, for 30 minutes. (You can allow the remaining stock to cool slightly.)

Transfer about half the soup to a food processor or blender and purée until smooth. Return this to the soup in the pan.

Put the rest of the stock and the leaves in the food processor or blender, and process for 1 minute. Add this liquid to the soup along with the peas, dill, and salt and pepper. Reheat gently.

Ladle the soup into bowls and swirl in a spoonful of your chosen cream. If you like, spoon some cooked rice into the soup as well.

CHLODNIK

SERVES 4

This is a beautiful pink and green chilled soup from
Poland, for which home-made stock is essential.
The soup is usually made with beetroot boiled or baked
until very soft, but I prefer raw or lightly steamed
beetroot. This undeniably needs more chewing but it
has a fresher taste and fewer nutrients are lost during
steaming. If your beets have been divested of their leaves,
use a handful of spinach, spring greens or Swiss chard
instead. Serve the soup with bowls of large peeled
prawns and quartered hard-boiled eggs, and some
dark rye bread or pumpernickel. Beetroot is an excellent
source of folate and it also contains a useful amount of
vitamin C.

*3 small raw beetroot, preferably with leaves, flesh peeled and
finely diced*
$^1/_2$ cucumber
4 spring onions, green parts included, chopped
*450 ml/16 fl oz Chicken Stock (page 188) or
Light Vegetable Stock (page 181)*
150 ml/$^1/_4$ pint buttermilk
2 tbsp chopped fresh dill
3 tbsp snipped fresh chives
1 tbsp lemon juice
salt and freshly ground black pepper

TO GARNISH
8 radishes, thinly sliced
lemon slices

Remove the stalks from the beet leaves, if available. Slice
the leaves into ribbons and place in a steamer basket set

over boiling water. If you want to steam the beetroot flesh instead of leaving it raw, add this at the same time. Steam for 5–7 minutes until just tender. Remove from the basket and allow to cool.

Slice the cucumber lengthways and scoop out the seeds. Cut crossways into thin slices and combine with the beetroot and leaves, spring onions, stock, buttermilk, herbs, lemon juice and seasoning. Chill well – about 3 hours. When ready to serve, garnish with the radishes and lemon slices.

CALDO VERDE

SERVES 4

A favourite rustic soup from Portugal. Leave out
the garlic sausage if you prefer a meatless version.
Serve with hunks of crusty bread.

2¹/₂ tbsp olive oil
1 onion, finely diced
1 garlic clove, finely chopped
450 g / 1 lb floury potatoes, cut into large chunks
1.4 litres / 2¹/₂ pints Chicken Stock (page 188) or
Vegetable Stock (page 180)
100 g / 3¹/₂ oz garlic sausage (optional), sliced
350 g / 12 oz dark green cabbage, such as cavalo nero, Savoy or
kale, tough stalks removed, leaves very finely sliced
1 tsp salt
¹/₂ tsp coarsely ground black pepper
Salsa Verde (page 226) or olive oil

Heat 2 tablespoons of the oil in a large saucepan and gently
fry the onion for 5 minutes until translucent. Add the
garlic and fry for another minute. Add the potatoes and
stock. Bring to the boil then simmer gently for about 20
minutes, until the potatoes are just beginning to break up.

Meanwhile, fry the sausage in the remaining oil for a few
minutes until crisp. Drain on paper towels.

Roughly mash the potatoes into the liquid. Mix in the
cabbage, salt, pepper and sausage. Simmer for 5–7 minutes
until the cabbage is tender. Check the seasoning before
serving.

Pour into bowls and swirl in some salsa verde or a good
slick of fruity olive oil.

BAKED POTATO AND CHEESE SOUP

SERVES 4–5

This soup is simple and supremely comforting –
just right for a winter evening, or if you're feeling
a bit low or over-stressed.

4 large baking potatoes
3 tbsp olive oil
2 onions, finely diced
2 garlic cloves, finely chopped
425 ml/³/₄ pint Chicken Stock (page 188) or
Vegetable Stock (page 180)
4 tbsp snipped fresh chives
¹/₄–¹/₂ tsp dried chilli flakes
100 ml/3¹/₂ fl oz single cream
salt and freshly ground black pepper
25 g/1 oz Cheddar cheese, finely grated
115 g/4 oz diced bacon lardons, fried until crisp

Bake the potatoes in a preheated oven at 200°C (190°C
fan oven)/gas 6 for 45 minutes until tender but not too soft.
Allow to cool, then remove and discard the skins. Cut the
flesh into 1 cm/¹/₂ inch cubes.

Heat the oil in a large saucepan and gently fry the onions
for 15 minutes until soft but not coloured. Add the garlic
and fry for another minute.

Stir in the stock, half of the diced potato, the chives and
chilli flakes. Bring to a simmer, stirring and mashing the
potato until smooth. Add the cream, and salt and pepper,
and stir until smooth. Check the seasoning.

Stir in the remaining potato cubes. Stir until heated
through but do not mash. Ladle into bowls and top with
grated cheese and crisply fried cubes of bacon.

MAJORCAN VEGETABLE SOUP

SERVES 6

This soup is substantial enough to eat on its own
but you could serve it with Catalan Tomato Bread
(page 208) if you like.

150 ml/¼ pint olive oil
2 leeks, green parts included, finely chopped
3 spring onions, green parts included, finely chopped
3 garlic cloves, finely chopped
200 g/7 oz can chopped tomatoes
½ tsp paprika
4 large cabbage leaves, tough stalks removed, leaves shredded
850 ml–1.2 litres/1½–2 pints Tomato Stock (page 183) or
Vegetable Stock (page 180)
115 g/4 oz green beans, chopped
85 g/3 oz shelled peas
115 g/4 oz spinach, shredded
sea salt and freshly ground black pepper
10 slices French bread

Heat 75 ml/3 fl oz of the oil in a pan over medium heat.
Add the leeks and spring onions and gently fry for a few
minutes until soft. Stir in the garlic and fry for another
minute.

Stir in the tomatoes and paprika, cook for a minute
or two then throw in the cabbage leaves and about
300 ml/½ pint stock. Stir everything around until the
cabbage begins to soften, then add the beans. Cover and
cook for 5 minutes, then add the peas and spinach with
another 150 ml/¼ pint of stock. Season, then cover and
cook again for about 5 minutes. By now, the vegetables
should be giving off their juices and there should be a fair
amount of liquid.

Drain the vegetables, reserving the cooking liquid. Put half the bread in the base of a 2.2 litre/4 pint ovenproof casserole and sprinkle with some of the oil. Spoon half the vegetables over and top with the rest of the bread and a bit more oil to moisten. Arrange the rest of the vegetables on top.

Pour in the cooking liquid and another 425 ml/¾ pint of stock. Add more liquid if you like, but the soup is intended to be quite dense. Drizzle with the last of the oil and place uncovered in a warm oven for 10 minutes to allow the flavours to blend.

MUSHROOM AND RED PEPPER SOUP WITH ALMOND AND GARLIC PICADA

SERVES 6

This is adapted from a recipe from the Spanish region of Catalan. A picada is a chunky pounded paste of garlic, nuts and usually parsley, sometimes with saffron, as here, or with other spices, and bread. The mixture adds rich substance to the soup. This is a particularly nourishing soup since the main ingredients contain significant amounts of a wide spread of nutrients. Mushrooms, especially shiitakes and chanterelles, have higher than usual levels of B vitamins, selenium and iron. Red peppers are packed with beta-carotene, lutein (another type of carotene) and vitamin C. Almonds contain huge amounts of vitamin E and magnesium, and are a good source of iron, calcium, zinc and B vitamins.

450 g / 1 lb mixed wild or cultivated mushrooms, such as
shiitakes, chanterelles or chestnut mushrooms
6 tbsp olive oil
2 onions, finely chopped
6 large tomatoes, peeled and chopped
1 red pepper, deseeded and finely diced
5 tbsp chopped fresh garlic chives or finely chopped spring onion
2 litres / 3$^{1}/_{2}$ pints Mushroom Stock (page 182) or
Chicken Stock (page 188), or a mixture
salt and freshly ground black pepper
6 slices ciabatta or French bread

FOR THE PICADA
2 garlic cloves
small pinch of saffron threads
200 g/7 oz almonds, toasted in the oven
salt

Cut the mushrooms into more-or-less equal-sized chunks. Heat 3 tablespoons of the oil in a frying pan. Add the mushrooms and gently fry for 7–10 minutes, until most of the liquid has evaporated. Remove from the heat and set aside.

Heat the remaining oil in a large saucepan. Add the onions and gently fry for about 5 minutes. Add the tomatoes, red pepper and 3 tablespoons of the garlic chives or spring onions. Continue to cook for another 5–8 minutes until the tomatoes and peppers are soft.

Add the mushrooms and the stock, and season. Bring to the boil, add the bread and simmer gently for 5 minutes.

Pound the picada ingredients to a chunky paste with a pestle and mortar or use a food processor. Mix with some of the soup liquid, then add to the pan. Simmer for another 5 minutes and then check the seasoning. Ladle into shallow soup plates and sprinkle with the remaining garlic, chives or spring onions.

BUTTERNUT SQUASH, TOMATO AND BLACK BEAN SOUP

SERVES 4–5

This colourful soup is an excellent source of carotene, vitamin C and E – antioxidants strongly implicated in protecting against certain cancers. Vegetarians can leave out the bacon and use vegetable stock (page 180) instead of chicken stock. Serve with plenty of good crusty bread.

500 g/1 lb 2 oz butternut squash, prepared as described on page 14 then cut into large chunks
115 g/4 oz streaky bacon, diced
2 tbsp light olive oil or sunflower oil
1 onion, diced
2 tsp chopped fresh rosemary
250 g/9 oz cooked black beans or
125 g/4¹/₂ oz uncooked black beans
400 g/14 oz can chopped tomatoes
700 ml/1¹/₄ pints Chicken Stock (page 188)
1 tsp sugar
salt and freshly ground black pepper
3 tbsp chopped fresh flat-leafed parsley
grated cheese, to garnish

Steam the squash over boiling water for 10 minutes, or microwave until just tender. Put the bacon in a saucepan with plenty of water. Bring to the boil, simmer for 10 minutes to remove excess salt, then drain.

Heat the oil in a large saucepan. Add the drained bacon and gently fry until lightly browned. Stir in the onion and rosemary, cover and cook gently for 5 minutes. Stir in the diced squash and the beans, and cook for a minute or two until heated through. Add the tomatoes, stock, sugar, and salt and pepper. Bring to the boil, then reduce the heat and simmer gently, covered, for 40 minutes.

Stir in the parsley. Ladle into shallow bowls and top with grated cheese.

WINTER VEGETABLE SOUP WITH DUMPLINGS

SERVES 6

A wonderfully rib-sticking soup, perfect for a weekend lunch. Use any of the suggested dumpling recipes, but I find the lemon pepper version particularly good. If you precook the dumplings, add them to the soup with the leek and cabbage. Add uncooked dumplings after the stock has boiled. Serve with chunks of cooked ham, crusty bread and some nice crumbly Wensleydale or Caerphilly cheese.

2 tbsp olive oil or extra-virgin sunflower oil
2 tsp dried oregano or thyme
1 large onion, quartered and thinly sliced
4 celery stalks, thinly sliced
4 carrots, thinly sliced
1 turnip, diced, or 175 g/6 oz diced swede
1 litre/1¾ pints Ham Hock Stock (page 191) or
Vegetable Stock (page 180)
Lemon Pepper, Cheese, or Bacon and
Onion Dumplings (page 220)
1 leek, green parts included, sliced
115 g/4 oz green cabbage, shredded
salt and freshly ground black pepper
chopped fresh parsley or chives, to garnish

Heat the oil with the oregano or thyme in a large heavy-based saucepan. Add the onion, celery, carrot and turnip. Cover and sweat over medium heat for 10 minutes.

Pour in the stock and bring to the boil. If using uncooked dumplings, add them now. Simmer for 5 minutes, then add the leek and cabbage (and precooked dumplings, if using). Season, and simmer for another 5 minutes before serving. Pour into individual bowls and garnish with fresh parsley or chives.

Soups with Pulses and Grains

Pulses and grains make the most deeply satisfying and flavour-ful soups. Naturally bland but far from boring, they team well with potent aromatics – fiery chillies, soy sauce, ginger, lime – and robustly flavoured vegetables such as garlic, tomatoes and onions. These complement the subtle mellowness of pulses and grains, which in turn smooth out and balance the stronger flavours.

Pulses and grains are also a rich source of carbohydrate and B vitamins, both of which boost energy levels, but they are conveniently low in fat so they satisfy the appetite without piling on the pounds.

The timeless quality of these most ancient of foods is surely reflected in the fact that there is hardly a country in the world where a hearty pulse- or grain-based soup does not feature as part of the traditional cuisine. Think of the thick bean and rice soups of Italy and Spain, the spicy dhal dishes of India, chilli-spiked Mexican bean soups, Middle Eastern lentil and chick-pea soups, split-pea soups from Eastern Europe and traditional British soups made with pearl barley.

With this wealth of inspiration it was hard to know where to stop but I have tried to include a wide enough range of recipes so that you can experience for yourself the enormous number of soups that can be made with pulses and grains. Then you will be able to go on to develop some of your own. Most of the soups can be kept in the fridge for several days and, indeed, taste even better the second time around.

THE RECIPES

BLACK BEAN, CHILLI AND TORTILLA SOUP WITH CORIANDER CREAM

SERVES 6

This is a great Mexican-style soup, full of strong earthy flavours. It makes a colourful spread served with Grilled Corn, Avocado and Tomato Salsa (page 228), some crumbled hard cheese such as Caerphilly or feta, and a salad of robust mixed green leaves. Supermarkets are beginning to sell named varieties of chillies, so you should be able to find Anaheims. They are quite large but not overly hot. Weight for weight, fresh chillies provide up to six times more beta-carotene than a tomato and thirteen times more vitamin C.

225 g / 8 oz black beans, soaked overnight
2–3 Anaheim chillies or other large fresh chillies
5 tbsp groundnut oil
6 small corn tortillas, broken into bite-sized pieces
1 onion, finely chopped
3 garlic cloves, finely chopped
450 g / 1 lb flavourful ripe tomatoes, peeled and chopped, or
400 g / 14 oz can chopped tomatoes
2 tbsp tomato purée
2 large fresh epazote sprigs (see page 240) or
oregano sprigs
700 ml / 1¼ pints Chicken Stock (page 188) or
Vegetable Stock (page 180)
1 tsp salt
freshly ground black pepper
5 tbsp chopped fresh coriander
Coriander Cream (page 231) or soured cream

Drain the beans, put in a saucepan and cover with fresh water. Bring to the boil, boil rapidly for 15 minutes, then continue to simmer briskly for 15–30 minutes until the beans are soft but still holding their shape. Drain and set aside.

While the beans are cooking, preheat the oven to 220°C (210°C fan oven)/gas 7. Place the chillies in a small roasting tin and roast in the preheated oven for 10–15 minutes until the skin begins to blister and blacken – do not over-roast, otherwise the flesh tends to disintegrate. When cool enough to handle, remove the seeds and peel off the skin. Put the chilli flesh in a blender with 2 tablespoons of water and purée until smooth. Scrape into a small bowl and set aside.

Heat 4 tablespoons of the oil in a large non-stick frying pan over medium–high heat. Add the tortilla pieces a few at a time and stir-fry for a few minutes, turning, until golden and crisp. Drain on paper towels.

Heat the remaining tablespoon of oil in a large saucepan. Add the onion and gently fry for 5 minutes until translucent. Add the garlic and fry for another minute. Then stir in the chilli purée, the tomatoes and their juices, tomato purée and epazote or oregano. Simmer over medium-low heat for 10 minutes, stirring now and then.

Next add the drained beans and the stock. Season with the salt and some freshly ground pepper, and simmer for 10 minutes more. Transfer two-thirds of the mixture to a food processor or blender and purée until smooth. Tip this back into the saucepan with the rest of the soup and reheat gently. Check the seasoning and stir in the coriander.

Divide the fried tortilla pieces between individual serving bowls. Ladle the soup over the tortillas and swirl in some coriander cream or soured cream.

BLACK BEAN, SQUASH AND SWEETCORN SOUP WITH ROASTED CHILLI CREAM

SERVES 6

Beans, squash and sweetcorn form a kind of holy trinity in the cooking of Central America. The combination is uniquely satisfying and packed with nutrients. Like all orange-fleshed fruit and vegetables, butternut squash contains extremely high levels of beta-carotene. Both squash and sweetcorn are an excellent source of vitamin C and folate. Serve with Chilli and Coriander Corn Muffins (page 210), tortillas or crusty bread.

200 g/7 oz black beans, soaked overnight
3 tbsp olive oil
1 tbsp paprika
2 red onions, finely chopped
3 garlic cloves, finely chopped
450 g/1 lb prepared weight butternut squash (see page 14 for preparation), cut into 2 cm/³/₄ inch cubes
400 g/14 oz can chopped tomatoes
700 ml/1¹/₄ pints Chicken Stock (page 188) or Vegetable Stock (page 180)
salt and freshly ground black pepper
225 g/8 oz frozen sweetcorn kernels or the kernels stripped from 2 large ears of corn
Roasted Chilli Cream (page 234) or soured cream
6 tbsp chopped fresh coriander

Drain the beans, put in a saucepan and cover with fresh water. Bring to the boil, boil rapidly for 15 minutes, then continue to cook at a brisk simmer for 15–30 minutes until soft but still holding their shape. Drain and set aside.

Heat the oil with the paprika in a large saucepan. Add the onions, cover and simmer gently for 10 minutes. Add the garlic, squash and tomatoes and cook for another 5 minutes.

Add the drained beans and pour in the stock. Season generously with salt and pepper and simmer for 15 minutes, adding more stock or water if necessary. Add the corn and cook for 3–5 minutes more.

Ladle into bowls, swirl in a blob of roasted chilli cream or soured cream, and sprinkle with the coriander.

RIBOLLITA

SERVES 6–8

For a truly authentic version of this gutsy Tuscan soup,
you really do need *cavalo nero* – a variety of dark green
Italian cabbage. It is easy to grow but fairly elusive in the
shops, although some supermarkets are now beginning
to stock it. You can use kale or Savoy cabbage instead
but do include the dark green outer leaves. It is not
absolutely essential to chill the soup overnight, but
the flavour will mature and improve
if you do so.

FOR THE BEANS
250 g/9 oz cannellini beans, soaked overnight
1 large tomato
1 celery stalk
6 garlic cloves, unpeeled
handful of fresh sage leaves
salt

FOR THE SOUP
6 tbsp olive oil
2 red onions, chopped
2 celery stalks, thinly sliced
2 carrots, chopped
200 g/7 oz can chopped tomatoes
2 garlic cloves, finely chopped
4 tbsp chopped flat-leafed parsley
1 tsp fresh thyme leaves
800 g/1 lb 12 oz cavalo nero, Savoy cabbage or
kale, tough stalks removed, leaves cut into thin strips
salt and freshly ground black pepper
1.2 litres/2 pints Chicken Stock (page 188),
Rich Meat Stock (page 190) or Vegetable Stock (page 180)

8 thick slices stale Italian bread
extra-virgin olive oil
sea salt flakes

First cook the beans: drain them, place in a saucepan and cover with fresh water. Bring to the boil, boil rapidly for 15 minutes, then drain again. Return to the pan and cover with fresh water by a depth of about 5 cm/2 inches. Add the tomato, celery, garlic and sage. Bring to the boil again, covered, then simmer for 30 minutes until the beans are tender but still holding their shape. Add salt and cook for another 5 minutes. Remove from the heat and leave the beans to stand in the cooking water, discarding the vegetables and sage.

While the beans are cooking, heat the oil in a large saucepan over medium heat. Add the onions, celery, carrots, tomatoes, garlic, parsley and thyme. Cover and gently fry for 45 minutes.

Add the cabbage, two-thirds of the beans and all their cooking water. Cover and simmer for 10 minutes until the greens have cooked down a bit, then add enough stock to just cover. Simmer for 50–60 minutes, adding extra stock if necessary. The mixture should be thick but still soupy. Purée the remaining beans and add to the pan. Season with salt and pepper. Allow to cool, then cover and leave in the fridge overnight.

Reheat the soup gently. Lay a slice of bread in the bottom of each serving bowl and ladle the soup over. Pour on a generous amount of extra-virgin olive oil – don't stint – and a sprinkling of sea salt flakes.

BORLOTTI BEAN AND RICE SOUP

SERVES 4–5

I am completely addicted to this soup – it's not
at all smart but it is flavourful, comforting and
undemanding. Serve with a simple tomato salad,
a few black olives and maybe some salami
on the side.

200 g/7 oz borlotti, red kidney or cranberry beans,
soaked overnight
2 tbsp olive oil
$^1/_2$ tsp fresh or dried thyme leaves
$^1/_2$ tsp dried oregano
1 onion, finely chopped
1 celery stalk, finely chopped
1 carrot, finely chopped
115 g/4 oz pancetta, rindless bacon or ham, chopped
4 large tomatoes, peeled and chopped
1 litre/1$^3/_4$ pints Ham Hock Stock (page 191),
Rich Meat Stock (page 190) or Vegetable Stock (page 180)
salt and freshly ground black pepper
115 g/4 oz risotto rice, such as arborio or carnaroli
4 tbsp chopped flat-leafed parsley
extra-virgin olive oil
freshly grated Parmesan cheese, to serve

Drain the beans, put in a saucepan and cover with fresh
water. Bring to the boil, boil rapidly for 15 minutes then
continue to cook at a brisk simmer until tender – this could
take up to an hour, depending on the type and age of the
beans. Drain and set aside.

Heat the oil in a large saucepan with the thyme and oregano. Add the onion and gently fry until pale golden. Add
the celery, carrot and pancetta, and cook, stirring now and

then, for about 10 minutes. Then pour in the tomatoes with their juices and simmer very gently for another 15 minutes.

Add the drained beans, stirring to coat, and cook for 5 minutes. Pour in the stock and season with salt and pepper. Cover, bring to a gentle boil, then add the rice – you may need to add more stock or water at this point since the soup needs to be liquid enough for the rice to cook. Cover and simmer for 10–15 minutes until the rice is tender but still has some bite.

Ladle into bowls, sprinkle with parsley, and dribble in some good olive oil. Serve the Parmesan cheese separately.

WHITE BEAN AND FENNEL SOUP WITH FENNEL AND PARSLEY GREMOLATA

SERVES 4–5

The mild aniseed flavour of fennel is perfect with creamy white beans. The gremolata, a finely chopped mix of fennel leaves or parsley, lemon zest and garlic, adds colour and brightens up the flavour, while a slick of olive oil and a sprinkling of Parmesan make for a seriously filling soup. Serve with Garlic Croûtons (page 209) or Catalan Tomato Bread (page 208). Fennel is a useful source of vitamin C and folate.

200 g/7 oz haricot or cannellini beans, soaked overnight
2 fennel bulbs, preferably with leaves
finely chopped flat-leafed parsley
2 tbsp olive oil
$^1/_2$ tsp fennel seeds, crushed
1 fresh bay leaf
2–3 thyme sprigs
1 onion, finely diced
1 celery stalk, quartered lengthways and finely diced
2 large tomatoes, peeled, deseeded and diced
1 litre/1$^3/_4$ pints Chicken Stock (page 188) or Tomato Stock (page 183)
salt and freshly ground black pepper
1 garlic clove, finely chopped
finely grated zest of $^1/_2$ lemon
extra-virgin olive oil
freshly grated Parmesan cheese, to serve

Drain the beans and put in a saucepan with fresh water to cover. Bring to the boil, boil rapidly for 15 minutes, then continue to cook at a brisk simmer for 30–45 minutes until the beans are tender. Drain and set aside.

If the fennel has leaves, trim and finely chop them and mix with enough chopped parsley to make 4 tablespoonfuls in all.

Trim the fennel bulbs, discarding the base and tough outer leaves. Cut into quarters and discard the central core. Thinly slice the flesh lengthways.

Heat the oil in a large saucepan with the fennel seeds, bay leaf and thyme. Add the onion, fennel and celery, cover and cook for 10 minutes until soft. Add the tomatoes, drained beans, stock, and salt and pepper to taste. Bring to the boil then simmer for 15 minutes.

While the soup is cooking, make the gremolata by combining the fennel leaf and parsley mixture with the garlic and lemon zest.

Ladle the soup into bowls and garnish with a spoonful of gremolata. Dribble in some olive oil and serve with grated Parmesan.

BLACK AND WHITE BEAN SOUP WITH RED PEPPER AND CHORIZO

SERVES 4–6

This hefty soup is an absolute winner, producing repeated requests for encores. It's worth doubling up the quantities and keeping some in the freezer. Chorizo sausage is highly seasoned so you won't need any salt and pepper. Serve with hot crusty bread or tortillas and Avocado and Chilli Sauce (page 227).

175 g/6 oz black beans, soaked overnight
90 g/3^1/$_2$ oz haricot beans, soaked overnight
^{1}/$_2$ tsp cumin seeds
1 tsp coriander seeds
1 tsp dried oregano
1 tbsp olive oil
1 onion, finely chopped
1 red pepper, deseeded and cut into 1 cm/^{1}/$_2$ inch squares
^{1}/$_2$ tsp dried chilli flakes
2 garlic cloves, very finely chopped
175 g/6 oz chorizo, thickly sliced
400 g/14 oz can chopped tomatoes
600 ml/1 pint Rich Meat Stock (page 190) or
Chicken Stock (page 188)
fresh coriander sprigs, to garnish

Drain the beans, put in separate saucepans and cover with fresh water. Bring to the boil, boil rapidly for 15 minutes, then continue to cook at a brisk simmer for another 30–45 minutes until the beans are soft but still holding their shape. Drain and set aside.

Put the cumin and coriander seeds in a small heavy-based pan without any oil, and dry-fry over medium heat until the seeds smell fragrant. Sprinkle in the oregano and fry for a few seconds. Immediately remove from the pan. Lightly crush with a pestle and mortar.

Heat the oil in a large saucepan and gently fry the onion and red pepper with the dry-fried spice mixture and the chilli flakes, if using. When the onion and pepper are soft, stir in the garlic and chorizo and cook for 2–3 minutes.

Pour in the chopped tomatoes and stock along with the drained beans. Bring to the boil and simmer for 30 minutes.

Ladle the soup into bowls and garnish with coriander sprigs.

DRIED AND FRESH BEAN SOUP WITH CHILLI AND RICE

SERVES 8

This is a really rustic, earthy soup – impossible to make in small quantities. It looks lovely if you use a colourful mixture of dried beans – get hold of some heritage varieties if you can. Serve in shallow soup plates with plenty of good bread and red wine. The soup contains a good range of vitamins and minerals, and plenty of carbohydrate and fibre.

225 g/8 oz dried mixed beans such as cannellini, black beans or appaloosa beans, soaked overnight
1.7 litres/3 pints Vegetable Stock (page 180) or water
3 celery stalks, thickly sliced
1 turnip, cut into chunks
350 g/12 oz Swiss chard or spinach, stalks included, sliced crossways into broad ribbons
1 small sweet potato, cut into bite-sized chunks
1 potato, cut into bite-sized chunks
3 tbsp olive oil
1 onion, finely diced
2 red peppers, finely diced
3–4 fresh red chillies, deseeded and finely diced
2 tsp salt
freshly ground black pepper
75 g/2¾ oz long-grain white rice
350 g/12 oz frozen or shelled fresh broad beans

Drain the beans, put in a large saucepan and cover with the stock or water. Bring to the boil, then boil for 15 minutes. Add the celery, turnip and half the chard. Cover and simmer over low heat for 30 minutes until the beans are tender.

(If you like, you can leave the mixture to cool at this stage and continue the next day.)

Next, add both kinds of potato to the pan, and bring back to the boil if you have allowed the mixture to cool.

Meanwhile, heat the oil in a frying pan and gently fry the onion, pepper and chillies until the onion is just starting to colour. Add the fried vegetables and the oil to the vegetable and bean mixture. Add the salt and plenty of freshly ground black pepper. Simmer over medium heat for 15 minutes.

Stir in the rice and simmer for 15 minutes, adding more water or stock if the mixture gets too thick – it should still be quite soupy.

Add the broad beans (no need to defrost) and the remaining chard and cook for 5 minutes more until the broad beans are just tender. Check the seasoning before serving.

CHICK-PEA AND GRILLED AUBERGINE SOUP WITH YOGURT AND MINT

SERVES 6

This is a delicious soup full of Middle-Eastern flavours –
earthy chick-peas, rich velvety aubergines, fragrant
spices, mint and cool yogurt. Serve it with a salad of Cos
lettuce hearts, tomato segments and cucumber chunks,
some warm pitta bread and, if you like, Lebanese Lamb
Balls (page 223). Chick-peas are one of my favourite
pulses. Not only do they taste good, but they are a
particularly good source of folate, potassium, iron and
magnesium. They also provide significant amounts of
calcium, vitamin E and B vitamins.

200 g/7 oz chick-peas, soaked overnight
1 aubergine, cut crossways into 2 cm/^{3}/$_4$ inch slices
3–4 tbsp olive oil
1 large onion, finely chopped
1 large red pepper, cut into 1 cm/^{1}/$_2$ inch squares
^{3}/$_4$ tsp ground cinnamon
^{1}/$_2$ tsp ground allspice
3 garlic cloves, finely chopped
400 g/14 oz can chopped tomatoes
finely grated zest of 1 lemon
1 litre/1^3/$_4$ pints Chicken Stock (page 188) or
Vegetable Stock (page 180)
salt and freshly ground black pepper
150 ml/^{1}/$_4$ pint plain yogurt
2 tbsp chopped fresh mint
1 large pitta bread
3 tbsp chopped flat-leafed parsley
cumin seeds, dry-fried, to garnish

Drain the chick-peas and put in a saucepan with plenty of fresh water to cover. Bring to the boil and boil rapidly for 15 minutes. Reduce the heat to a brisk simmer and continue to cook for about another 25–35 minutes until tender. Drain and set aside.

While the chick-peas are cooking, arrange the aubergine slices in a single layer in a non-stick grill pan. Brush lightly with oil and grill for 10–12 minutes, turning once, until beginning to blacken. Cut into bite-sized segments.

Heat the remaining oil in a large saucepan over medium heat. Add the onion and red pepper, sprinkle with the cinnamon and allspice, and gently fry for 5–7 minutes until soft. Add two-thirds of the garlic and fry for another minute or two. Add the aubergines, drained chick-peas, tomatoes, lemon zest, stock, and salt and pepper to taste. Bring to the boil, then simmer gently for 20 minutes.

Meanwhile, mix the yogurt with the mint, the remaining garlic and a little salt.

Open out the pitta bread and toast in a warm oven until crisp. Break the bread into bite-sized pieces and place in the bottom of serving bowls.

Stir the parsley into the soup and check the seasoning. Ladle the soup over the bread. Add a spoonful or two of yogurt and sprinkle with dry-fried cumin seeds.

FARRO SOUP

SERVES 4

Farro, as the Italians call it, or spelt, is an ancient grain similar to pearl barley. You can buy farro in healthfood shops and, now that it is considered a 'smart' grain, in speciality food shops. Serve the soup with some good cheese and a green salad for a satisfying main meal.

175 g/6 oz farro, soaked in cold water for 2 hours
sea salt flakes
2 tbsp olive oil
1 tbsp finely chopped fresh rosemary
75 g/2³/₄ oz pancetta or unsmoked bacon, finely diced
¹/₂ red pepper, deseeded and finely diced
¹/₂ red onion, finely diced
2 celery stalks, quartered lengthways and finely diced
2 garlic cloves, finely chopped
1 small potato, diced
freshly ground black pepper
850 ml/1¹/₂ pints Chicken Stock (page 188) or
Rich Meat Stock (page 190)
50 g/1³/₄ oz cooked borlotti beans or drained, canned beans
50 g/1³/₄ oz cooked cannellini or drained, canned beans
4–8 thick slices of Italian bread, toasted in a warm
oven until hard
extra-virgin olive oil

Drain the farro and put in a saucepan with plenty of fresh water to cover. Add 1 teaspoon of sea salt flakes, cover and bring to the boil. Reduce the heat and simmer for 35 minutes until tender, stirring now and again to prevent sticking. Drain, reserving the liquid.

While the farro is cooking, heat the oil with the rosemary in a large saucepan over medium heat. Put in the pancetta and gently fry for 3–4 minutes. Add the red pepper, onion, celery and garlic, and cook for 2 minutes. Then add the potato and cook for 5 minutes more until the vegetables are softened. Season with sea salt and pepper. Pour in the stock, then cover and simmer for 15 minutes.

When the vegetables are tender, add the farro to the pot along with the beans and enough of the farro cooking liquid to make a thick soupy mixture. Continue to cook for 15 minutes. Check the seasoning.

Place one or two slices of toasted bread in the bottom of each soup bowl and ladle the soup over. Drizzle with olive oil before serving.

WILD RICE, MUSHROOM AND HAZELNUT SOUP

SERVES 4

This is a richly flavoured and filling soup which needs
only a big green salad and ciabatta bread to go with
it. Wild rice has a deliciously nutty flavour and
contains more protein than brown or
white long-grain rice. It is a good source
of carbohydrate and fibre.

90 g/3¹/₂ oz wild rice
salt
2 tbsp olive oil
1 tbsp fresh thyme leaves
225 g/8 oz mushrooms, such as chestnut, flat cap and
shiitake, finely chopped
425 ml/³/₄ pint Vegetable Stock (page 180),
Chicken Stock (page 188) or Mushroom Stock (page 182)
2 carrots, coarsely grated
4 spring onions, green parts included, finely chopped
5 tbsp hazelnuts, toasted in the oven and chopped
¹/₄ tsp freshly ground black pepper
150 ml/¹/₄ pint single cream
4 tbsp chopped parsley
diced cooked ham or bacon, to serve

Put the rice in a saucepan with enough water to cover by
the depth of your thumbnail. Add 1 teaspoon of salt, bring
to the boil, then cover and simmer over very low heat for
45–50 minutes until tender.

Heat the oil with the thyme in a large saucepan. Add
the mushrooms, and fry for 7–10 minutes. Pour in the stock
and bring to the boil. Add the rice, carrots, spring onions,

nuts and pepper with enough extra stock or water to cover if necessary.

Simmer for 5 minutes, then stir in the cream and reheat gently. Stir in the parsley and check the seasoning. Pour into bowls and add some diced cooked ham or bacon.

MIXED BEAN AND GRAIN SOUP WITH GREEN BEANS, TOMATOES AND SWEETCORN

SERVES 6

The combination of beans, lentils and rice means you'll be getting plenty of good quality plant protein as well as fibre and carbohydrate to boost energy levels. Serve with Cheese Toasts (page 206), or, if you want a really substantial soup, any of the Three Meat Balls (page 222).

*115 g/4 oz mixed beans and brown or
green lentils, soaked overnight
75 g/2³⁄₄ oz mixed brown and wild rice or
200–225 g/7–8 oz cooked rice
salt
2 tbsp sunflower or safflower oil
1 tsp dried oregano
¹⁄₂ tsp dried chilli flakes
1 small onion, finely diced
1 celery stalk, leaves included, quartered lengthways
and finely diced
175 g/6 oz green beans, cut into 1 cm/¹⁄₂ inch pieces
4 tomatoes, peeled, deseeded and chopped
1 litre/1³⁄₄ pints Chicken Stock (page 188) or
Vegetable Stock (page 180)
kernels from 1 large sweetcorn ear, or
115 g/4 oz frozen kernels
freshly ground black pepper
3 tbsp chopped fresh coriander or flat-leafed parsley*

Drain the beans and lentils, put in a saucepan and cover with fresh water. Bring to the boil, boil rapidly for 15 minutes then continue to cook at a brisk simmer for another 20–30 minutes until tender but not mushy. Drain and set aside.

While the beans and lentils are cooking, put the rice in a saucepan with enough water to cover by the depth of your thumbnail. Add 1 teaspoon of salt, bring to the boil, then cover and simmer over very low heat for 45–50 minutes until the rice is cooked.

Heat the oil in a large saucepan with the oregano and chilli flakes. Add the onion, celery, green beans and tomatoes, then cover and cook over medium-low heat for a few minutes. Pour in the stock, bring to the boil and add the cooked beans and lentils, and the rice. Cover and simmer for 10 minutes. Add the sweetcorn kernels, season with pepper and cook for 5 minutes more. Check the seasoning and stir in the coriander or parsley just before serving.

LEBANESE LENTIL AND SPINACH SOUP

SERVES 6

Tiny purple-brown Puy lentils have a distinctive earthy flavour, far superior to other brown or green lentils. They are an excellent source of vitamin B6, folate and selenium, an important trace mineral. They also contain useful amounts of zinc and iron. You can buy them in large supermarkets and healthfood shops. If you don't have any tomato stock, purée a 400 g/14 oz can of chopped tomatoes and add sufficient water to make it up to 1 litre/1¾ pints.

175 g/6 oz Puy lentils
1 onion, finely diced
1 litre/1¾ pints Tomato Stock (page 183)
¹/₂ tsp salt
¹/₂ tsp cumin seeds, dry-fried
2–3 potatoes, diced
350 g/12 oz spinach, stalks removed, leaves
cut into thin ribbons
1 tbsp lemon juice
3 tbsp chopped fresh mint
freshly ground black pepper
3 pitta breads
6 tbsp Greek yogurt
3–4 tbsp chopped fresh mint
a few dry-fried cumin seeds
lemon wedges, to garnish
extra-virgin olive oil

Put the lentils in a saucepan with the onion, tomato stock, salt and cumin seeds. Bring to the boil then simmer, covered, for 20 minutes.

Add the potatoes and cook for 10 minutes, then throw in the spinach and cook for another 10 minutes. If necessary, add more water or stock at this stage to make the soup soupier – but it should still be fairly thick. Stir in the lemon juice and mint, and season with freshly ground black pepper.

Meanwhile, open the pitta breads out flat and toast in the oven until crisp. Break into bite-sized pieces and arrange round the edge of six soup plates. Ladle the soup into the middle. Add a blob of yogurt, a little chopped mint and some dry-fried cumin seeds. Garnish with a lemon wedge. A dribble of peppery, golden-green olive oil – Lebanese if possible – adds the finishing touch.

LENTIL AND BULGAR WHEAT SOUP WITH GARLIC, MINT AND LEMON

SERVES 4

Soups made with grains and pulses often need perking up with a touch of something zesty and piquant. Thinly sliced lemon and a tempering of sizzling oil, garlic and mint do the job perfectly. Serve with Lemon and Mint Turkey Balls (page 222) or Tomato, Mint and Rice Stuffed Leaves (page 217).

2 onions, thinly sliced
175 g/6 oz Puy lentils
75 g/2³⁄₄ oz bulgar wheat
1 tbsp tomato purée
1.7 litres/3 pints Chicken Stock (page 188),
Rich Meat Stock (page 190) or Vegetable Stock (page 180)
salt and freshly ground black pepper
1 tsp ground cumin
juice of 1 lemon
4 tbsp olive oil
3 garlic cloves, very finely chopped
6 tbsp chopped fresh mint
4 very thin lemon slices, to garnish
Greek yogurt, to serve

Put the onions, lentils, bulgar wheat, tomato purée and stock in a large saucepan. Bring to the boil, then simmer gently for 30 minutes until the lentils are very tender. If using turkey balls, add them after 20 minutes of cooking. Season with salt and pepper to taste, and stir in the cumin and lemon juice.

Heat the oil in a small frying pan. Add the garlic and mint and fry for 30 seconds until the garlic is just starting to colour.

Ladle the soup into bowls. Pour in the garlic-mint mixture including the oil, and garnish with a slice of lemon. If
using stuffed cabbage leaves, serve while still warm in a
separate dish. Serve with a bowl of thick Greek yogurt.

COUSCOUS SOUP
WITH ROASTED VEGETABLES

SERVES 6–8

This is a real main meal soup, just slightly soupier than ordinary couscous – fragrant broth, soft and mild couscous grains, tasty chunks of roasted vegetables, and piquant harissa sauce. Harissa is a fiery red paste of chillies and spices, available from Middle Eastern food shops and large supermarkets. Serve with Lebanese Lamb Balls (page 223) and Stuffed Eggs (page 214) or quartered hard–boiled eggs.

1 aubergine, thickly sliced crossways
2 courgettes, halved lengthways
olive oil
2 red and 1 yellow peppers, halved and deseeded
6 baby onions, preferably purple, peeled and left whole
2 small turnips, quartered
3 tomatoes, peeled and quartered
225 g/8 oz green cabbage, cut into wedges
1.7 litres/3 pints Chicken Stock (page 188) or
Vegetable Stock (page 180)
3 garlic cloves, crushed
1 tsp salt
¹/₂ tsp freshly ground black pepper
1 tsp cinnamon
¹/₂ tsp ground ginger
¹/₄ tsp ground allspice
350 g/12 oz couscous
225 g/8 oz peeled and deseeded butternut squash or pumpkin,
cut into 2.5 cm/1 inch cubes
8 tbsp chopped fresh coriander
8 tbsp chopped fresh flat-leafed parsley
¹/₂ tsp harissa sauce

Preheat the oven to 220°C (210°C fan oven)/gas 7. Lightly brush the aubergine slices and courgettes with oil. Place in a roasting tin with the peppers, cut side down. Use two tins if necessary – don't overcrowd the vegetables otherwise they will steam in their own moisture instead of developing nice crusty black bits. Roast in the preheated oven, turning the aubergine slices and courgettes, for about 20 minutes until beginning to blacken.

When cool enough to handle, remove the skin from the peppers and cut the flesh into 2.5 cm/1 inch squares. Cut the courgettes into large chunks, and the aubergine slices in half. Set aside.

Put the onions, turnips, tomatoes and cabbage in the bottom of a couscousière or a large saucepan over which a steamer basket or colander will fit. Pour in the stock and add the garlic, salt, pepper and spices. Bring to the boil and simmer for about 25–30 minutes until the vegetables are just tender. You can remove the pan from the heat at this stage and continue cooking when you're about ready to serve.

Meanwhile, soak the couscous in warm water for 10 minutes. Put in the top section of the couscousière, or a muslin-lined steamer basket or sieve.

Bring the vegetables back to the boil and add the squash or pumpkin, and the lamb balls, if using. Fit the couscous container over the pan making sure the bottom does not touch the vegetables. Cover and steam for 10 minutes. Then add the roasted peppers and courgettes to the other vegetables, and continue cooking with the couscous container in place until heated through. The vegetables should be quite soupy. Stir in the coriander and parsley.

To serve, put the couscous in a wide shallow dish, fluffing the grains with a fork. Make a well in the centre and ladle in the vegetables with some of the liquid. Mix the harissa sauce with 2–3 ladlefuls of cooking liquid and serve in a jug. Pour the remaining liquid into a jug or bowl so that people can help themselves.

Alternatively, ladle the vegetables and their liquid into bowls or soup plates, and serve the couscous separately.

CHICK-PEA, COURGETTE AND ROSEMARY SOUP WITH ROASTED PEPPER CREAM

SERVES 4

Served with Cheese Toasts (page 206), Bruschetta (page 207) or Grilled Polenta (page 212), this is a substantial, well-balanced soup made colourful by lightly cooked courgettes and a swirl of roasted pepper cream.

200 g/7 oz chick-peas, soaked overnight
1 tbsp olive oil
1 tbsp finely chopped fresh rosemary
1 onion, chopped
450 g/1 lb tomatoes, peeled and chopped
1.3 litres/2¼ pints Chicken Stock (page 188) or
Vegetable Stock (page 180)
salt and freshly ground black pepper
2 small courgettes, coarsely grated
Roasted Pepper Cream (page 225)
extra-virgin olive oil

Drain the chick-peas, put in a saucepan with plenty of fresh water to cover. Bring to the boil, boil rapidly for 15 minutes, then drain.

Heat the oil with the rosemary in a large saucepan. Add the onion and cook gently, covered, for 10 minutes. Add the drained chick-peas, tomatoes and their juice, and stock. Bring to the boil, then simmer for 1–1¼ hours until the chick-peas are tender. Add salt and pepper once they have begun to soften.

Add the courgettes and simmer for 2 minutes more (the courgettes should still be bright green when served). Check the seasoning and ladle the soup into bowls. Swirl in the pepper cream and dribble over a bit of olive oil.

SPLIT-PEA AND BACON SOUP

SERVES 6

Split-peas are, I think, sadly under-used. They are every bit as tasty as the more popular chick-peas and Puy lentils. Combined with bacon and earthy root vegetables they make a mellow base to this wholesome winter soup. Serve with hunks of dark rye bread and perhaps a salad of shredded cabbage, carrots and dill.

2 tbsp grapeseed or sunflower oil
1 onion, finely chopped
2 carrots, finely chopped
1 celery stalk with leaves, finely sliced
1 large potato, diced
275 g/9$^{1}/_{2}$ oz yellow split-peas, soaked overnight, rinsed and drained
1 fresh bay leaf
400 g/14 oz can chopped tomatoes
850 ml/1$^{1}/_{2}$ pints Ham Hock Stock (page 191) or Chicken Stock (page 188)
pinch ground cloves
freshly ground black pepper
225 g/8 oz piece smoked bacon, fat removed, diced
1 tbsp finely chopped fresh sage
chopped fresh sage or Sizzled Sage (page 235), to garnish

Heat the oil in a large saucepan over medium heat. Add the onion, carrots and celery, and cook for about 5 minutes until beginning to soften.

Add the potato, split-peas, bay leaf, tomatoes, stock and ground cloves. Season with plenty of freshly ground pepper. Bring to the boil, then cover and simmer very gently for 2–2$^{1}/_{2}$ hours.

When the peas are very soft, add the bacon and the sage.

Simmer for another 30 minutes, adding water or stock if the mixture starts to get too thick for your liking. Check the seasoning.

Ladle into big bowls and scatter with some fresh or crispy sizzled sage.

DHAL SOUP WITH CARROTS AND CASHEW NUTS

SERVES 3-4

Split-peas or lentils spiked with chillies, ginger and spices make deliciously sloppy, soup-like dishes known as dhal. They are simple to prepare and immensely comforting. This version contains carrots and cashew nuts added for colour and crunch. Asafoetida is a vile-smelling yellow powder which, when cooked, is transformed to a fragrant aromatic redolent of mushrooms and onions. Don't worry if you don't have any, the soup will survive without it. Serve with yogurt and some warm naan bread or pappadums.

4 tbsp sunflower or safflower oil
2.5 cm / 1 inch piece fresh ginger root, very finely chopped
1 fresh green chilli, deseeded and finely chopped
$1/2$ tsp ground turmeric
1 tbsp coriander seeds, crushed
4 carrots, thinly sliced
200 g / 7 oz yellow split-peas, soaked overnight, rinsed and drained
1 litre / $1^3/4$ pints boiling Vegetable Stock (page 180) or water
$1/2$ tsp salt
3 tbsp chopped fresh coriander or flat-leafed parsley
50 g / $1^3/4$ oz cashew nuts
1 tsp cumin seeds
$1/2$ tsp asafoetida powder (optional)

Heat 1 tablespoon of the oil in a large saucepan. Add the ginger, chilli, turmeric and coriander seeds. Fry for a few seconds to flavour the oil. Add the carrots and cook, covered, over gentle heat for 5 minutes.

Add the split-peas to the pan with the boiling stock or water. Bring back to the boil, then cover and simmer over low heat for about 45 minutes until the peas are soft and beginning to break up. Mash with the back of a wooden spoon to thicken the liquid. Remove from the heat and stir in the salt and fresh coriander or parsley.

Heat the remaining oil in a small heavy-based frying pan. Add the cashew nuts and fry until pale golden. Remove with a perforated spoon, chop roughly, and stir into the soup.

Add the cumin seeds to the oil remaining in the pan and fry until they start to colour. Sprinkle with the asafoetida, if using, and remove from the heat. Pour into the soup, cover and leave to stand for a few minutes while the flavours are absorbed.

SPICY DHAL AND ROASTED PEPPER SOUP

SERVES 4–5

This is a delicious mix of soupy split-peas and roasted sweet peppers spiked with chillies, lemon juice and fresh coriander. A tempering of sizzling fragrant spices adds the finishing touch. Serve with Lacy Chick-Pea Pancakes (page 204) or pappadums.

1 small green pepper, halved and deseeded
1 small red pepper, halved and deseeded
4 tbsp sunflower or safflower oil
1/2 tsp mustard seeds
1 small onion, finely chopped
1 tomato, peeled and chopped
1–2 fresh green chillies, deseeded and finely chopped
2 garlic cloves, finely chopped
1/2 tsp ground turmeric
1/2 tsp paprika
200 g/7 oz yellow split-peas, soaked overnight and drained
1 litre/1³/4 pints boiling Vegetable Stock (page 180) or water
1 tsp salt
2 tbsp lemon juice
4 tbsp chopped fresh coriander
10 black peppercorns, crushed
4 cloves, crushed
seeds from 4 green cardamom pods, crushed

Preheat the oven to 220°C (210°C fan oven)/gas 7. Put the peppers in a small roasting tin, cut side down, and roast in the preheated oven for 15–20 minutes until beginning to blacken. Allow to cool then peel off the skin and chop the flesh into neat 1 cm/1/2 inch squares. Set aside.

Heat 1 tablespoon of the oil in a large saucepan and add the mustard seeds. When they begin to pop, throw in the onion, tomato, chilli and garlic. Cook, stirring, for a few minutes until softened, then stir in the turmeric and paprika.

Add the drained split-peas and the boiling stock to the pan. Bring to the boil, then simmer over low heat, covered, for 45–50 minutes or until mushy. Use the back of a wooden spoon to break up the peas.

Stir in the peppers, salt, lemon juice and coriander, and cook for 2–3 minutes more. Remove from the heat.

Heat the remaining oil in a small heavy-based frying pan. When almost smoking, add the peppercorns, cloves and cardamom seeds. Sizzle for a few seconds until fragrant, then pour into the soup. Cover and leave to stand for a few minutes to absorb the flavours.

MUNG BEAN AND LEAFY GREEN SOUP

SERVES 4

Mung beans are tiny, round, dried green beans with a lovely sweetish flavour. They contain relatively high levels of a wide range of minerals and vitamins, including potassium, magnesium, iron, zinc, selenium and B vitamins, and are widely used in traditional Chinese and Indian ayurvedic medicine to cure a variety of ills. With the leafy greens, high in beta-carotene, this is a power-packed soup. Serve with Stuffed Eggs (page 214) and Lacy Chick-Pea Pancakes (page 204) or naan bread, and a bowl of creamy yogurt.

200 g/7 oz mung beans, soaked for 1 hour
1 tsp ground turmeric
2 tsp coriander seeds, crushed
2 cm/³/₄ inch piece fresh ginger root, very finely chopped
1 small fresh red or green chilli, deseeded and chopped (optional)
1 litre/1³/₄ pints Vegetable Stock (page 180) or water
150 g/5¹/₂ oz shredded spinach, Swiss chard, kale or beet greens, tough stalks removed
1 tsp salt
1 tbsp lemon juice
1 tbsp sunflower or safflower oil
¹/₂ tsp cumin seeds
4 cloves, slightly crushed
seeds from 3 cardamom pods, crushed
pinch of asafoetida powder (optional)

Drain the beans and put in a large saucepan with the turmeric, coriander seeds, ginger and chilli, if using. Add the stock and bring to the boil. Cover and cook over medium heat for 30 minutes, then add the greenery and salt. Cook for another minute or so, until the leaves have wilted but are still bright green. Remove from the heat and stir in the lemon juice.

Heat the oil in a small heavy-based frying pan until almost smoking. Add the cumin seeds, cloves and cardamom and sizzle for a few seconds until fragrant. Sprinkle with the asafoetida powder, if using, and cook for just a second or two. Add the hot spice mix to the soup, cover and leave to stand for a few minutes to absorb the flavours.

WHEAT GRAIN, LEEK AND CARROT SOUP

SERVES 4

You can buy whole wheat grains (wheat berries) in healthfood shops. They have a lovely nutty flavour and a pleasantly chewy texture. The soup is delicious with Latkes (page 211) or Cheese Toasts (page 206).

115 g/4 oz whole wheat grains, soaked overnight
850 ml/1¹/₂ pints Chicken Stock (page 188) or
Vegetable Stock (page 180)
2 tbsp olive oil
3 leeks, green parts included, finely sliced
3 carrots, finely diced
2 celery stalks, quartered lengthways and finely diced
salt and freshly ground black pepper
5 tbsp snipped fresh chives
3 tbsp crème fraîche
115 g/4 oz diced bacon lardons, fried until crisp (optional)

Drain the wheat and put in a saucepan with 200 ml/7 fl oz of the stock and enough water to cover by at least 2.5 cm/ 1 inch. Bring to the boil then cover tightly, reduce the heat to a simmer, and cook for about 55 minutes until the grains are tender. Drain and set aside.

Heat the oil in a large saucepan. Add the leeks, carrot and celery, cover and cook over medium heat for 5–7 minutes until the vegetables are just tender but still brightly coloured.

Stir in the drained wheat and the remaining stock. Bring to the boil, then cover and simmer over medium-low heat for 10 minutes. Season with salt and pepper, then remove from the heat and stir in the chives and crème fraîche. Ladle into bowls and top with the fried lardons, if using.

Noodle Soups

Since the earliest days of civilisation, noodle soups have been one of the world's staples, lifting the spirits and providing a nourishing source of energy-giving carbohydrate, B vitamins and minerals.

The term 'noodles' includes types as diverse as Italian wheat flour pasta, Central European flour and egg noodles, Japanese soba noodles made with buckwheat, Chinese egg thread noodles, and the glutinous rice noodles of Southeast Asia. Noodles come in strings and strands, broad and narrow ribbons, coiled nests and all manner of shapes, lending themselves to a wonderful variety of soups.

This chapter demonstrates their versatility and includes hearty minestrones and delicately flavoured Japanese soups along with spicy concoctions from Thailand and Vietnam.

THE RECIPES

MEXICAN VERMICELLI SOUP

SERVES 4

This is a hearty soup full of zinging flavours. You will not want to eat again for several hours. Serve with warm tortillas.

2 tomatoes, roughly chopped
1 garlic clove, finely chopped
2 tbsp finely diced onion
1 tbsp groundnut oil
1.2 litres/2 pints Chicken Stock (page 188)
115 g/4 oz vermicelli, broken into short lengths
1 small fresh red chilli, deseeded and finely sliced
225 g/8 oz baby kale or spinach, tough stems removed, leaves roughly chopped
salt and freshly ground pepper
3–4 tbsp chopped fresh coriander
150 g/5^1/$_2$ oz feta or Wensleydale cheese, cubed
Roasted Garlic Cream (page 234), Roasted Chilli Cream (page 234) or soured cream
finely diced red onion, to garnish

Purée the tomatoes, garlic and onion in a blender. Heat the oil in a small saucepan, add the purée and stir-fry over medium-high heat for about 3 minutes until reduced. Set aside.

Bring the stock to the boil in a large saucepan, add the vermicelli and chilli and cook for 5 minutes. Next, add the kale or spinach and the tomato mixture. Cover and simmer for 5–8 minutes until the vermicelli is tender. Season with salt and pepper, and stir in the coriander.

Put the cheese in the bottom of individual bowls. Ladle the soup over and add a dollop of your preferred cream. Sprinkle with diced red onion.

COURGETTE AND PASTA SOUP WITH ITALIAN BEEF BALLS

SERVES 6

This is one of those undemanding homely soups that make a much-appreciated mid-week supper. If your beef balls are already made and sitting in the freezer, so much the better. If there's no time to make them from scratch, use chunks of left-over Sunday roast or cooked ham instead. You can vary the vegetables as well. Serve with Cheese Toasts (page 208) or Bruschetta (page 209), and a green salad.

2 tbsp olive oil
1 onion, finely chopped
2 celery stalks, thinly sliced
2 carrots, halved lengthways and sliced
2 tsp dried oregano
2 tsp chopped fresh rosemary
2 garlic cloves, finely chopped
400 g/14 oz can chopped tomatoes
1–1.2 litres/1³/₄–2 pints Rich Meat Stock (page 190) or
Chicken Stock (page 188)
Italian Beef Balls (page 222)
salt and freshly ground black pepper
150 g/5¹/₂ oz pasta shells such as conchiglie or orecchiette
1 courgette, thinly sliced
3 tbsp chopped flat-leafed parsley
freshly grated Parmesan cheese

Heat the oil in a large saucepan over medium heat. Add the onion, celery, carrots and herbs, and sweat, covered, for 10 minutes. Add the garlic and tomatoes, and cook for 5 minutes more.

Pour in 1 litre/1³/₄ pints of the stock, add the meatballs

and season to taste. Bring to the boil, then reduce the heat, cover and simmer for 30 minutes.

Raise the heat to a gentle boil. Add the pasta and cook for 15–20 minutes, adding more stock if necessary. When the pasta is *al dente*, add the courgette and cook for a few minutes until tender but still crisp and brightly coloured. Check the seasoning.

Pour into bowls and sprinkle with the parsley. Serve with plenty of Parmesan cheese.

TORTELLONI IN BRODO

SERVES 6

Home-made tortelloni cooked in a richly flavoured meat broth is one of the most delicious and comforting soups imaginable. You can, of course, use ready-made tortelloni, but should you feel like devoting a morning to making your own, here is the recipe. There will be left-over stuffing but this can be frozen until you next get the urge to make tortelloni. Serve with ciabatta bread and a large salad of mixed green leaves.

1.7 L/3 pints Rich Meat Stock (page 190)
fresh basil, shredded
freshly grated Parmesan cheese, to serve

PASTA DOUGH
200 g/7 oz plain flour (preferably Italian '00')
2 eggs (at room temperature), lightly beaten

STUFFING
2 tbsp olive oil
75 g/2³/₄ oz pork fillet, diced
75 g/2³/₄ oz skinless, boneless chicken breast, diced
25 g/1 oz mortadella sausage, very finely chopped
150 g/5¹/₂ oz ricotta cheese
1 egg yolk
50 g/1³/₄ oz Parmesan cheese, freshly grated
salt and freshly ground black pepper

To make the pasta dough, pour the flour on to the work surface, make a well in the centre and add the beaten eggs. Using a fork, gradually incorporate the flour from the inside of the well into the egg, until the egg is thickened and no longer runny. Then, using both hands, quickly sweep the remaining flour over the egg mixture and work together until evenly mixed. The dough should feel moist but not sticky. Knead for 10–15 minutes until very smooth and springy. Wrap in clingfilm and leave to rest for 30 minutes.

To make the stuffing, heat the oil in a frying pan and stir-fry the pork for 5 minutes until evenly browned. Remove with a perforated spoon and leave to cool. Add the chicken and fry for 2 minutes. Put the pork, chicken and remaining stuffing ingredients in a food processor and blend to a coarse purée.

Divide the pasta dough into quarters. Working with one piece at a time and keeping the rest covered, roll out the dough until paper thin using a machine or elbow grease. Cut into 7.5 cm/3 inch squares. Place a teaspoon-sized ball of stuffing in the centre of each square. Moisten the edges of the dough and fold into triangles, pressing the edges to seal.

Working with one triangle at a time, moisten the long points. With the tip of the triangle uppermost, wrap the triangle round the back of your index finger, overlapping the long points, and press to seal. Remove from your finger, form into a round shape and place upright on a clean cloth, making sure the tortelloni do not touch.

Bring the stock to the boil and toss in a few tortelloni. Cook over high heat for 2–3 minutes, then, using a perforated spoon, transfer them to a warm tureen. When all the tortelloni are in the tureen, pour the boiling stock over and sprinkle with plenty of fresh basil. Serve at once with a bowl of freshly grated Parmesan.

SPRING MINESTRONE

SERVES 6

The flavour of minestrone improves if made the day
before, so if you have time, leave the soup overnight after
you have cooked the first lot of vegetables and before
adding the pasta. Bring back to the boil before adding
the reserved green vegetables. Minestrone is traditionally
served warmish or at room temperature rather than
piping hot – pour into bowls and leave to stand for
a few minutes before serving.

3 tbsp extra-virgin olive oil
1 large onion, very thinly sliced
2 carrots, finely diced
1 celery stalk, quartered lengthways and finely diced
1 potato, diced
2 garlic cloves, finely chopped
200 g/7 oz can chopped tomatoes
4 tbsp roughly chopped fresh herbs such as flat-leafed parsley,
lovage, thyme and chives
4–5 basil leaves, shredded
175 g/6 oz French beans, chopped
175 g/6 oz asparagus, tough stems discarded, tips and tender
stems cut into 5 cm/2 inch pieces
175 g/6 oz shelled young broad beans
115 g/4 oz courgettes, finely diced
115 g/4 oz shredded dark green cabbage
1 litre/1³/4 pints Chicken Stock (page 188) or
Vegetable Stock (page 180)
salt and freshly ground black pepper
25 g/1 oz small pasta shapes such as stelline
115 g/4 oz cooked or drained canned haricot beans
2 tbsp freshly grated Parmesan cheese

TO GARNISH
shredded basil leaves
extra-virgin olive oil

TO SERVE
thickly sliced ciabatta or French bread
freshly grated Parmesan cheese

Heat the oil in a large saucepan. Add the onion and cook over medium-low heat for 15 minutes until pale golden. Add the carrots, celery, potato, garlic, tomatoes, half the chopped herbs and half the basil. Cook for 5 minutes, then add half the green vegetables and cook for another 5 minutes. (Keep the reserved vegetables in a plastic bag in the fridge.) Pour in the stock and season with salt and pepper. Cover and simmer very gently for $1\frac{1}{2}$–2 hours.

Raise the heat to a more vigorous simmer, stir in the pasta and haricot beans and cook for 10 minutes. Then add the reserved green vegetables and cook for another 5 minutes. Check the seasoning. Just before serving, stir in the Parmesan and all the remaining herbs.

Place slices of bread in individual serving bowls. Ladle the soup over the bread, then leave to stand for 5 minutes. Garnish with shredded basil and a good slick of olive oil. Serve with plenty of freshly grated Parmesan.

WINTER MINESTRONE

SERVES 4–5

This is a reasonably quick version of the Italian classic.
Serve with plenty of freshly grated Parmesan cheese, and,
if you like, a slick of Pesto Sauce (page 226).

3 tbsp extra-virgin olive oil
1 onion, thinly sliced
50 g/1¾ oz rindless bacon, finely diced
2 garlic cloves, finely chopped
200 g/7 oz can chopped tomatoes
2 tbsp roughly chopped fresh herbs, such as flat-leafed parsley,
sage, marjoram, thyme
1 celery stalk, thinly sliced
1 carrot, diced
75 g/2¾ diced turnip
1 leek, sliced
75 g/2¾ oz peeled celeriac, diced
salt and freshly ground black pepper
850 ml/1½ pints Ham Hock Stock (page 191) or
Chicken Stock (page 188)
50 g/1¾ oz cooked or canned drained haricot beans
50 g/1¾ oz short macaroni or small pasta shapes
115 g/4 oz frozen peas
2 tbsp freshly grated Parmesan cheese
thickly sliced ciabatta or French bread

Heat the oil in a large saucepan and gently fry the onion
and bacon over medium-low heat, stirring occasionally, until
the onion is just golden. Add the garlic, tomatoes and herbs.
Cook for 5 minutes to a sauce-like consistency.

Add the rest of the vegetables. Cover and sweat for 5
minutes. Season with salt and pepper. Pour in the stock,
bring to the boil, then simmer, covered, for 30 minutes.

Add the beans and pasta, and simmer for about 15 minutes until the pasta is cooked. Check the seasoning, stir in the peas and cook for 5 minutes more. Just before serving, stir in the Parmesan.

Place slices of bread in individual serving bowls, pour the soup over the bread and leave to stand for a few minutes.

SOBA NOODLE SOUP WITH WATERCRESS, CARROT, DAIKON AND SPRING ONION

SERVES 4–5

This is a lightish but restoring soup, perfect for when you're feeling fragile. We call it Hangover Soup, which speaks for itself. To make the soup a little more substantial, add some Oriental Fish Dumplings (page 221) or serve it with Omelette Chunks (page 213). Soba noodles are egg-free and made with buckwheat. They are light and easy to digest, and provide useful carbohydrate to stabilise blood sugar levels after a night of over-indulgence. You can buy them in healthfood shops or large supermarkets.

75 g/2³/₄ oz soba noodles, cut into short lengths
1 litre/1³/₄ pints Oriental Vegetable Stock (page 186) or
Vegetable Stock (page 180)
150 g/5¹/₂ oz very finely diced carrot
150 g/5¹/₂ oz finely diced daikon (white radish)
8 spring onions, green parts included, sliced diagonally into
1 cm/¹/₂ inch pieces
115 g/4 oz watercress, stalks removed, leaves roughly chopped
2 tsp shoyu or tamari (Japanese soy sauce)
freshly ground black pepper
lemon juice, to taste
1 tsp sesame seeds, dry-fried, to garnish

To prepare the noodles, bring a large pan of water to the boil. Add the noodles a few at a time to avoid clumping. Bring back to the boil and skim off any scum that rises to the surface. Cook for 8 minutes until soft or according to packet instructions. Drain, rinse well with cold water and set aside.

Bring the stock to the boil. Add the carrot, daikon and spring onions. Boil for 3–4 minutes until just tender, then add the watercress and noodles. If you're including fish dumplings, add them now. Stir until heated through and the watercress has just wilted.

Season with shoyu or tamari, black pepper and a squeeze of lemon juice to sharpen the flavour. Ladle into bowls and sprinkle with the dry-fried sesame seeds.

RICE NOODLE AND TOFU SOUP WITH SHIITAKE MUSHROOMS AND MANGETOUT

SERVES 4–5

Although light, this nutrient-packed soup makes a well-balanced, satisfying meal. Serve it with a bowl of plainly cooked rice. Shiitake mushrooms are rich in amino acids, the building blocks which make up protein, and they are a good source of B vitamins. They are considered a potent medicine in traditional oriental healing, while modern research suggests they may help to inhibit the growth of viruses, reduce blood cholesterol levels and fight cancer.

3 tbsp grapeseed or sunflower oil
115 g/4 oz shiitake mushrooms, cut into thin strips
1–2 fresh red chillies, deseeded and thinly sliced
6 spring onions, green parts included, sliced diagonally into 1 cm/^{1}/$_2$ inch pieces
2 cm/^{3}/$_4$ inch piece fresh ginger root, very finely chopped
2 garlic cloves, very finely chopped
2 tbsp shoyu or tamari (Japanese soy sauce)
100 ml/3^1/$_2$ fl oz rice wine or dry sherry
1 litre/1^3/$_4$ pints Oriental Vegetable Stock (page 186) or Light Vegetable Stock (page 181)
25 g/1 oz rice noodles, cut into short lengths
175 g/6 oz firm tofu, drained thoroughly and cut into 2 cm/^{3}/$_4$ inch cubes
75 g/2^3/$_4$ oz mangetout
200 g/7 oz bok choy, leaves shredded, stalks cut into small squares
freshly ground black pepper
2 tbsp lemon juice
1 tbsp dark sesame oil

Heat the oil in a large saucepan. Add the mushrooms, chillies, spring onions, ginger and garlic, and fry gently until the mushrooms are tender.

Add the shoyu or tamari, rice wine and stock. Bring to the boil, add the noodles, then cover and simmer for 5–7 minutes.

Stir in the tofu, mangetout and bok choy, and cook for 5 minutes. Season with pepper, then stir in the lemon juice and sesame oil. Cook for 1 minute more until the vegetables are just tender but still brightly coloured. Serve at once.

VIETNAMESE NOODLE SOUP WITH CHICKEN AND ORIENTAL GREENS

SERVES 4

Like most oriental noodle soups, this one is immensely satisfying without overtaxing the system, and it is packed with health-promoting nutrients. Ginger adds a warming quality and aids digestion. Bok choy and kale contain amazingly high levels of carotenes and are an excellent source of vitamin C and folate. They also contain calcium, magnesium, iron and zinc.

1 litre/1¾ pints Chicken Stock (page 188) or
Chinese Stock (page 189)
3 skinless chicken breasts with bone, weighing
about 175 g/6 oz each
2.5 cm/1 inch piece fresh ginger root, coarsely chopped
3 garlic cloves
6 tbsp chopped fresh coriander
6 tbsp chopped fresh mint
115 g/4 oz shiitake mushrooms, sliced
2 tbsp groundnut oil
115 g/4 oz rice noodles
300 g/10 ½ oz bok choy, leaves shredded, stems diced
115 g/4 oz baby kale or mustard greens, roughly chopped
4 spring onions, green parts included, chopped
salt
chilli sauce, to taste
dry-fried sesame seeds, to garnish

Pour the stock into a large saucepan and bring to a gentle simmer over medium heat. Add the chicken breasts, ginger, garlic and half the coriander and mint. Simmer, covered, for about 30 minutes until the chicken is cooked.

While the chicken is cooking, fry the mushrooms in the oil for 5 minutes, and set aside. Soak the noodles in hot water for 5–10 minutes until softened. Drain and chop into shorter lengths. Plunge them into a large saucepan of boiling water and cook for 5–8 minutes until tender. Drain again, rinse under cold running water and set aside.

When the chicken is cooked, remove from the pan with a perforated spoon and tear into chunks, discarding the bones.

Strain the stock and return it to the pan. Add the bok choy and kale, and simmer over low heat for a few minutes until wilted.

Return the chicken to the pan along with the noodles, spring onion and mushrooms. Simmer for another minute until heated through. Add the remaining coriander and mint, and season to taste with salt. Pour into bowls, season with a dash of chilli sauce and garnish with sesame seeds.

THAI BEEF AND NOODLE SOUP

SERVES 4

This is a hearty protein-packed soup, brimming with wonderful oriental flavours – ginger, lime leaves, lemon grass, chillies, coriander and basil. With the exception of lime leaves, found mainly in oriental food shops, the ingredients are all available from larger supermarkets.

1.2 litres/2 pints Chinese Stock (page 189) or
Rich Meat Stock (page 190)
350 g/12 oz lean sirloin steak
5 cm/2 inch piece fresh ginger root, roughly chopped
2 garlic cloves
2 lime leaves (optional)
2 stalks lemon grass, bruised
2 tsp fish sauce (nuoc mam)
6 tbsp roughly chopped fresh coriander
6 tbsp roughly chopped Thai holy basil, or ordinary sweet basil
115 g/4 oz flat rice noodles
2 tbsp groundnut oil
4 shallots, thinly sliced
115 g/4 oz bean sprouts
6 spring onions, green parts included, thinly sliced, white and green parts kept separate
6 fresh Thai red chillies, deseeded and thinly sliced
1 lime, cut into wedges

Pour the stock into a large saucepan and bring to a gentle simmer over medium heat. Add the beef, ginger, garlic, lime leaves if using, lemon grass, fish sauce and half the coriander and basil. Cover and simmer for about 20 minutes.

Meanwhile, soak the noodles in hot water for 5–10 minutes until softened. Drain and chop into shorter lengths. Plunge into a large saucepan of boiling water and cook for 5–8 minutes until tender. Drain, rinse under cold running water and set aside.

Heat the oil in a frying pan over medium heat. Add the shallots and fry for 5–7 minutes until golden. Drain on paper towels.

Remove the beef from the saucepan with a perforated spoon and slice thinly.

Strain the stock, return it to the saucepan and bring to a simmer. Add the bean sprouts, white spring onion and chillies, and simmer for 2–3 minutes.

Return the beef to the pan with the noodles, green spring onion and fried shallots, and simmer for a minute until heated through. Add the remaining coriander and basil. Pour into bowls and garnish with lime wedges.

EGG NOODLE, SWEETCORN AND CHICKEN SOUP

SERVES 4–6

This Chinese-style soup seems deceptively light, but it is in fact quite filling. However, if you're really hungry, serve it with some Omelette Chunks (page 213).

90 g/3¹/₂ oz thin egg noodles
2 sweetcorn ears or 200 g/7 oz frozen sweetcorn kernels
6 spring onions
3 boneless, skinless chicken breasts, weighing about
175 g/6 oz each
1 litre/1³/₄ pints Chinese Stock (page 189) or
Chicken Stock (page 188)
1 carrot, cut into matchsticks
1 small fresh red or green chilli, deseeded and thinly sliced
75 g/2³/₄ oz shelled fresh or frozen peas
salt and freshly ground black pepper
shoyu or tamari (Japanese soy sauce), to taste

Cook the noodles according to the packet instructions. Drain, cut into 10 cm/4 inch lengths and set aside.

Cut the kernels off the sweetcorn cobs. Slice the white part of the spring onions and cut the green part into shreds, setting the green part aside for garnish later. Cut the chicken into bite-sized chunks.

Pour the stock into a saucepan, add the carrot, chilli and chicken and bring to the boil. Cover and simmer gently for 5 minutes.

Add the corn, white spring onion and peas. Simmer, uncovered, for 3 minutes. Add the cooked noodles and simmer for another minute. Season with salt and pepper and pour into individual bowls. Garnish with the shredded green spring onion and season with shoyu or tamari.

Fish Soups

All countries with a coastline have created a repertoire of mouth-watering fish soups. This chapter draws upon cuisines as diverse as the Caribbean, Scotland and Japan, and includes classics such as Provençal Fish Soup and Cullen Skink, as well as more modern creations.

Fish and shellfish make excellent main meal soups, verging on soupy stews depending on the amount of liquid added. The best types of fish to use are dense-fleshed white varieties – oily fish such as trout or salmon would be too strongly flavoured for a soup. Use the freshest fish possible, taking care not to overcook it. If possible, avoid reheating fish soup. Not only will the texture suffer but there is a risk of food poisoning from harmful bacteria.

White fish and shellfish are a good source of protein and valuable minerals – calcium, iron and zinc – and they contain hardly any fat. Shellfish also provide the B vitamins needed for the release of energy from food within the body. Because fish are low in carbohydrate and vitamin C, many of these soups include root vegetables and leafy greens to compensate. Served with additional bread and a salad, they make a well-balanced meal.

THE RECIPES

CULLEN SKINK

SERVES 4–6

This is based on a classic Scottish soup made with the
excellent smoked Finnan haddock, traditionally sold on
the bone. You can use any other smoked white fish but
preferably not the lurid yellow, artificially smoked type. If
the fish has already been filleted, you will need about
500g/1 lb 2 oz. Serve with thickly sliced and buttered
wholemeal bread or soda bread.

*800 g/1 lb 12 oz floury potatoes, such as Pentland Squire,
Maris Piper or King Edward, cut into chunks
1 onion, finely diced
500 ml/18 fl oz milk
500 ml/18 fl oz Chicken Stock (page 188)
2 Finnan haddock on the bone, about 900 g/2 lb
50 g/1³/₄ oz butter
salt and freshly ground black pepper*

TO GARNISH
*hard-boiled eggs (optional)
4 tbsp snipped fresh chives*

Put the potatoes and onion in a large saucepan with
the milk and stock. Bring to the boil then simmer for 10
minutes. Place the fish on top of the potatoes, cover and
simmer for 5 minutes more until the fish is just cooked.

Using a perforated spoon, lift the fish out of the pan into
a shallow dish. Remove the skin and bones and flake the
flesh. Roughly mash the potatoes into the liquid in the pan.
Mix in the flaked fish, adding the butter and plenty of
seasoning.

Ladle into bowls, top with hard-boiled egg segments if
you like, and sprinkle with chives.

PRAWN AND RED PEPPER BISQUE

SERVES 4

This is a smooth richly flavoured soup with a beautiful rosy colour. Serve with Aïoli (page 230), Stuffed Eggs (page 214), plenty of good crusty bread and a green salad. Recent research suggests that prawns, although high in cholesterol themselves, do not raise cholesterol levels in the blood. It is foods with a high saturated fat content that send your cholesterol levels shooting up and prawns contain very little of any kind of fat.

40 g/1$^1/_2$ oz unsalted butter
1 red pepper, halved deseeded and finely diced
50 g/1$^3/_4$ oz finely diced onion
2 potatoes, diced
2 tbsp each of finely diced carrot and celery
1 large garlic clove, very finely chopped
1 fresh bay leaf
450 g/1 lb uncooked shelled prawns
1 large tomato, deseeded and finely diced
1 litre/1$^3/_4$ pints Shellfish Stock (page 197) or
Fish Stock (page 196)
$^1/_2$ tsp salt
$^1/_2$ tsp freshly ground black pepper
$^1/_4$ tsp cayenne pepper

TO GARNISH
2 spring onions, green parts included, finely chopped
Garlic Croûtons (page 209)

Melt half the butter in a saucepan over medium–high heat. Add half the red pepper (save the rest as a garnish), the onion, potato, carrot, celery, garlic and bay leaf. Gently fry for 10 minutes, stirring occasionally, until lightly browned.

While the vegetables are cooking, melt the remaining butter in a frying pan over medium-high heat. When it's foaming, add the prawns and stir-fry for about 5 minutes until browned. Set aside twenty prawns. Transfer the rest to a food processor and process to a paste.

Deglaze the prawn pan with 3 tablespoons of stock and add the liquid to the vegetables. Stir in the tomato and cook for a few minutes until thickened.

Pour the remaining stock into the saucepan and add the prawn paste, salt, pepper and cayenne pepper. Bring to the boil then simmer gently for 15 minutes. Discard the bay leaf. Purée again, then push through a fine-meshed sieve back into the saucepan, pressing with the back of a wooden spoon to extract as much liquid as possible.

Add the reserved prawns and reheat very gently. Check the seasoning and serve, sprinkled with the spring onion, croûtons and reserved red pepper.

PROVENÇAL FISH SOUP WITH ROUILLE

SERVES 8

A home-made fish stock is vital for this soup, as is a good assortment of fish. Use dense-fleshed white fish rather than flaky fish such as cod and haddock. Also to be avoided are oily varieties such as salmon and mackerel. Rouille (page 224) is a rich, rust-coloured sauce made with pounded chillies, garlic, saffron, breadcrumbs and egg yolk. It is the traditional accompaniment to fish dishes in Provence. Serve the soup with a big green salad, extra French bread and some good cheese.

2.25 kg/5 lb assorted dense-fleshed white fish, such as whole red snapper, red mullet and sea bream, monkfish tail, shark and halibut steaks
1 fennel bulb, preferably with leaves, coarsely chopped
2 onions, finely sliced
400 g/14 oz can chopped tomatoes
6 garlic cloves, 4 crushed, 2 left whole
2 fresh jalapeño chillies, deseeded and chopped
100 ml/3¹/₂ fl oz Pernod
100 ml/3¹/₂ fl oz dry white wine
seeds from 2 star anise pods, crushed
1 tsp crumbled saffron threads
1 fresh bay leaf
2–3 thyme sprigs
1 large stale baguette, cut into 2 cm/³/₄ inch thick slices
8 tbsp olive oil
350 g/12 oz new potatoes, thickly sliced
16 mussels, cleaned and bearded
2.5 litres/4¹/₂ pints boiling Fish Stock (page 196)
salt and freshly ground black pepper
Rouille (page 224)

Clean the fish, discarding the heads and fins from the whole fish. You should be left with about 1.6 kg/3 lb 8 oz of prepared fish. Cut whole fish crossways into 6 cm/2½ inch thick cutlets. Cut fish steaks into 5 cm/2 inch pieces.

Put the prepared fish in a bowl and add the fennel, onions, tomatoes, crushed garlic and chillies, together with the Pernod, white wine, star anise, saffron, bay leaf and thyme. Stir well and leave to marinate in the fridge for at least 2 hours, or preferably overnight. Drain the fish, reserving the vegetables, herbs and liquid.

About 45 minutes before you're ready to serve the soup, preheat the oven to 180°C (170°C fan oven)/gas 4. Arrange the bread on a baking sheet and toast for about 10 minutes until golden. Rub with the whole garlic cloves while still warm and set aside.

Pour half the oil into a large saucepan or casserole. Add the vegetables and herbs from the marinade, and the potatoes. Arrange the biggest and thickest fish pieces on top, followed by the smaller pieces and finally the mussels.

Pour in the liquid from the marinade, the stock and the remaining oil, and season with salt and pepper. Cover and bring to the boil over high heat. After about 3 minutes start checking the fish. As each piece becomes cooked, remove it and place in a shallow serving dish. The mussels will be first (discard any that haven't opened), then the smaller chunks and finally the cutlets.

Continue boiling until the potatoes are cooked, then transfer them to the serving dish. Strain the vegetables and soup left in the pot, discarding the vegetables. Reheat the soup if necessary.

Place slices of bread smeared with rouille in the base of shallow soup plates and pour the soup over. Moisten the fish and potatoes with the remaining liquid and serve at the same time.

RED SNAPPER AND CHILLI CHOWDER

SERVES 6–8

Red snapper has a meaty flesh with a sweetish flavour which combines well with the sweetness of the corn and squash. Chillies add a touch of fire. Chilli and Coriander Corn Muffins (page 210) make a delicious accompaniment. If you're really hungry, serve some Black Bean Salsa (page 228) as well.

3 tbsp grapeseed oil or safflower oil
1 tsp cumin seeds, dry-fried
1 tsp dried oregano
1 small white onion, finely chopped
1 garlic clove, very finely chopped
2–3 fresh red or green chillies, deseeded and finely chopped
1–2 potatoes, cut into chunks
1 sweetcorn ear, cut into 2.5 cm/1 inch rounds and then halved lengthways
225 g/8 oz peeled butternut squash, cut into 2 cm/³⁄₄ inch squares
1.2 litres/2 pints Chicken Stock (page 188)
salt and freshly ground black pepper
550 g/1 lb 4 oz red snapper fillets, cut into chunks
125 g/4¹⁄₂ oz fresh or frozen peas
125 ml/4 fl oz milk or single cream
3 tbsp chopped fresh coriander

Heat the oil with the cumin and oregano in a large saucepan over medium heat. Add the onion, garlic and chillies, and stir-fry for 1 minute. Reduce the heat slightly and add the remaining vegetables. Cover and cook for 10 minutes until softened.

Pour in the stock and season generously with salt and pepper. Cover and simmer for 20 minutes until the vegetables are tender.

Add the red snapper fillets, peas and milk, and cook, uncovered, for 5 minutes more. Check the seasoning and stir in the coriander just before serving.

SEAFOOD SOUP WITH RED PEPPERS AND FENNEL

SERVES 6

This is a gutsy Mediterranean-style soup, brimming with chunks of vegetables, meaty fish and olives. Serve with Aïoli (page 230) and some French bread or Bruschetta (page 207). For a really substantial meal add a bowl of Chick-Pea and Feta Salsa (page 229).

2 red peppers, halved and deseeded
3 tbsp olive oil
1 onion, cut into 1 cm/^{1}/$_2$ inch pieces
1 fennel bulb, layers separated and cut into
1 cm/^{1}/$_2$ inch squares
1 tbsp fresh thyme leaves
2 large garlic cloves, very finely chopped
225 g/8 oz waxy new potatoes, halved
425 ml/^{3}/$_4$ pint Fish Stock (page 196)
425 ml/^{3}/$_4$ pint Chicken Stock (page 188)
1 tbsp tomato purée
400 g/14 oz can chopped tomatoes
50 g/1^3/$_4$ oz stale breadcrumbs
salt and freshly ground black pepper
500 g/1 lb 2 oz firm white fish fillets, cut into
2.5 cm/1 inch pieces
3 tbsp chopped fresh parsley

TO GARNISH
12 pitted black olives, halved
torn basil leaves

Preheat the oven to 230°C (fan oven 220°C)/gas 8. Roast the pepper, cut side down, for 15 minutes, until beginning to blacken and blister. When cool enough to handle, peel off the skin and chop the flesh into 1 cm/$\frac{1}{2}$ inch squares.

Heat 1 tablespoon of the oil in a large saucepan. Add the onion, fennel and half the thyme. Cover and gently fry over medium-low heat for 7 minutes until soft. Add the garlic and cook for another minute.

Next add the potatoes, stocks, tomato purée and tomatoes. Bring to the boil. Reduce the heat and simmer for 15 minutes until the potatoes are tender.

Meanwhile, heat the remaining oil in a frying pan over medium-high heat. Add the breadcrumbs and remaining thyme and season with salt and pepper. Fry, stirring frequently, until the breadcrumbs are golden and crunchy. Set the pan aside.

Add the peppers and fish to the soup in the pan and season to taste. Simmer for 5–7 minutes until the fish is just cooked. Stir in the parsley. Ladle the soup into bowls and top with a tablespoon of the breadcrumb mixture. Garnish with the olives and basil.

SEAFOOD SOUP WITH SAFFRON CREAM

SERVES 6

This is delicious with Saffron Cream (page 233), but you could use Roasted Garlic Cream (page 234) or Rouille (page 224) instead. Serve with plenty of French bread and a big green salad. Mussels and prawns are an excellent source of selenium – a vital trace mineral – and they also provide significant amounts of iron and zinc.

900 g/2 lb mussels, cleaned and bearded
1 fresh bay leaf
3 thyme sprigs
6 parsley sprigs
425 ml/³/₄ pint dry white wine
425 ml/³/₄ pint water
2 tsp olive oil
2 onions, diced
8 new potatoes, cut into chunks
2 celery stalks, sliced
1 red pepper, halved, deseeded and diced
1 garlic clove, finely chopped
200 g/7 oz can chopped tomatoes
300 ml/¹/₂ pint Fish Stock (page 196)
salt and freshly ground black pepper
650 g/1¹/₂ lb firm white fish, such as halibut, cod or snapper, cut into chunks
225 g/8 oz cooked tiger prawns, peeled
3 tbsp chopped flat-leafed parsley
cooked unpeeled prawns, to garnish

Put the mussels in a large heavy-based saucepan with the herbs, wine and water. Cook, tightly covered, over high heat for 5 minutes until the shells open, shaking the pan occasionally. Strain the cooking liquid through a muslin-lined sieve and reserve. Discard any mussels that have not opened. Remove the rest from their shells and reserve.

Heat the oil in a large saucepan. Gently fry the onions, potatoes, celery and pepper for 10–12 minutes. Add the garlic and tomatoes and fry for another minute or two.

Next, add the fish stock and mussel liquid. Bring to the boil and simmer over gentle heat for 15–20 minutes until the potatoes are tender. Season to taste with salt and pepper.

Add the fish chunks and simmer for 3 minutes more. When the fish is nearly cooked, stir in the mussels, prawns and parsley. Cook for a few minutes until heated through. Transfer to a large serving bowl and top with the unpeeled prawns.

CALLALOO WITH PRAWNS

SERVES 6

This soup is a classic from the eastern Caribbean, named after the main ingredient, callaloo – leaves of root vegetables such as taro, dasheen or eddoe. Traditionally, the actual roots are not used in the soup but I have included them to make it more substantial. Although Caribbean root vegetables are relatively easy to find in Europe, they are not generally sold with the leaves attached. However, you can use Swiss chard, kale or spinach instead. This soup is rich in carbohydrate and beta-carotene. It is delicious served with a dish of Lime-Thyme Cream (page 232) alongside.

2 tsp safflower or sunflower oil
1 onion, cut into 1 cm/^{1}/$_2$ inch squares
3 garlic cloves, finely chopped
225 g/8 oz trimmed spinach, Swiss chard or
callaloo leaves, cut into ribbons
225 g/8 oz kale, cut into ribbons
4 spring onions, green parts included, thickly sliced
550 g/1 lb 4 oz potatoes, yams, sweet potatoes, dasheens,
taro root or eddoes, cut into 1 cm/^{1}/$_2$ inch cubes
125 g/4^1/$_2$ oz okra, trimmed and thickly sliced
1 fresh green chilli, deseeded and finely chopped
^{1}/$_4$ tsp ground cloves
^{1}/$_4$ tsp ground cinnamon
600 ml/1 pint Chicken Stock (page 188) or
Vegetable Stock (page 180)
250 ml/9 fl oz coconut milk
salt and freshly ground black pepper
225 g/8 oz large shelled cooked prawns

TO GARNISH
lime wedges
finely diced red pepper
whole cooked prawns, unshelled

Heat the oil in a large saucepan, add the onion and gently fry until soft, then add the garlic and fry for another minute. Moisten with a little stock if necessary.

Next, add the remaining vegetables, the chilli, cloves and cinnamon. Cover and sweat over medium-low heat for 15 minutes, then pour in the stock and coconut milk. Season to taste with salt and pepper. Bring to the boil, then reduce the heat and simmer, covered, for 30–40 minutes until the root vegetables are soft.

Pour all but one-third of the mixture into a blender, purée to the desired consistency and then pour it back into the pan. Thin with a little stock or water if the soup is too thick for your liking.

Add the prawns to the pan and check the seasoning. Simmer until thoroughly heated through.

Pour into bowls and garnish with wedges of lime, diced red pepper and whole prawns. Serve with lime-thyme cream.

MUSSEL AND POTATO SOUP

SERVES 4

This soup reminds me of holidays in France. The flavour is delicious, particularly with a piquant cream or sauce swirled in. Serve with Catalan Tomato Bread (page 208), Bruschetta (page 207) or Cheese Toasts (page 206).

1.6 kg/3½ lb mussels, cleaned and bearded
1 litre/1¾ pints water
1 onion, chopped
4 garlic cloves, chopped
3 parsley sprigs
3 rosemary sprigs
1 fresh bay leaf
¼ tsp black peppercorns
350 g/12 oz waxy new potatoes, sliced
3 large tomatoes, deseeded and finely diced
salt
Roasted Garlic Cream (page 234), Aïoli (page 230) or
Rouille (page 224), to serve
snipped fresh chives, to garnish

Put the mussels in a large heavy-based saucepan with 225 ml/8 fl oz of the water. Cook, tightly covered, over high heat for 5 minutes until the shells open, shaking the pan occasionally. Strain the cooking liquid through a muslin-lined sieve and reserve. Discard any mussels that have not opened. Set aside 8–12 mussels in their shells. Remove the rest from their shells.

Put the remaining water in a saucepan with the onion, garlic, parsley, rosemary, bay leaf and peppercorns. Bring to the boil, then simmer, partially covered, for 30 minutes. Strain the infusion and mix with the mussel cooking liquid. Return the liquid to the pan and add the potatoes. Simmer for 15 minutes until the potatoes are cooked.

Add the diced tomatoes and the mussels, including those in their shells. Season, then simmer until the mussels are heated through. Ladle into warmed bowls, swirl in your chosen cream and garnish with chives.

PRAWN, CORN, CHILLI AND TORTILLA SOUP

SERVES 4

This is a soup with vibrant Mexican flavours – lime, chillies, and coriander – offset by the sweetness of the prawns and corn. Serve with Black Bean Salsa (page 228) or Chilli and Coriander Corn Muffins (page 210).

2 fresh green chillies
4 small corn tortillas, halved and cut into thin strips
1 tbsp olive oil
1 large onion, finely chopped
4 garlic cloves, finely chopped
2 large tomatoes, peeled, deseeded and chopped
$^1/_2$ tsp paprika
1 litre/1$^3/_4$ pints Shellfish Stock (page 197) or Chicken Stock (page 188), or a mixture
250 g/9 oz large uncooked shelled prawns
200 g/7 oz fresh or frozen sweetcorn kernels
sea salt and freshly ground black pepper
3 tbsp chopped fresh coriander
lime wedges, to serve

Preheat the oven to 230°C (220°C fan oven)/gas 8. Roast the chillies for 10 minutes until the skin begins to blacken and blister. When cool enough to handle, remove the skin and seeds, and cut the flesh into thin strips.

Reduce the oven temperature to 170°C (160°C fan oven)/gas 3. Place the tortilla strips on a baking sheet and toast for 5–8 minutes until crisp.

Heat the oil in a large saucepan, add the onion and cook, covered, over medium-low heat for 5 minutes until soft.

Add the garlic and cook for another minute. Add the toma-toes, raise the heat and cook, uncovered, until the liquid has almost evaporated, stirring often. Sprinkle with the paprika and cook for a few seconds more.

Pour in the stock and bring to the boil. Then add the prawns, sweetcorn and roasted chilli. Reduce the heat and simmer for a few minutes until the prawns are pink. Season with sea salt and black pepper.

Ladle the soup into bowls, pile the tortilla strips in the middle and sprinkle with coriander. Serve with lime wedges.

ORIENTAL SEAFOOD SOUP WITH ENOKI MUSHROOMS AND NOODLES

SERVES 4

Packed with carbohydrate, vitamins and minerals, this soup will have you coming back for more. Enoki mushrooms have pin-sized heads and grow in fascinating little clumps. They are available from larger supermarkets. Use ordinary mushrooms or shiitakes if you can't find any. Udon and soba noodles are available from healthfood shops.

2 litres/3$\frac{1}{2}$ pints Fish Stock (page 196)
2 slices fresh ginger root
1 Thai chilli
2 tender stalks lemon grass, bruised
sea salt and freshly ground black pepper
150 g/5$\frac{1}{2}$ oz udon or soba noodles
175 g/6 oz spinach, cut into ribbons
115 g/4 oz enoki mushrooms, root stump removed
225 g/8 oz monkfish or firm white fish, cut into cubes
150 g/5$\frac{1}{2}$ oz large shelled prawns
snipped garlic chives, to garnish

Put the stock in a large saucepan with the ginger, chilli and lemon grass. Bring to the boil, then simmer for 15 minutes. Season to taste with sea salt and black pepper. Using a perforated spoon, remove the vegetables and discard.

Bring the stock back to the boil and add the noodles. Cook for 5 minutes or according to the packet instructions, until just tender but still with a bit of bite. Drain, returning the stock to the pan. Cut the noodles into short lengths and set aside.

Bring the stock to the boil again. Add the spinach and mushrooms. Simmer for 5 minutes until just tender, then add the monkfish and prawns. Simmer for 5 minutes more until the fish is cooked.

Divide the noodles between four warmed bowls. Ladle the soup over the top, making sure everyone gets some fish and prawns. Garnish with garlic chives – including the flowers if you have any.

CATALAN FISH SOUP WITH GARLIC AND ALMONDS

SERVES 4

This is a lovely rich soup strictly for garlic lovers.
Serve with Catalan Tomato Bread (page 208), Bruschetta
(page 207) or any good crusty bread.

500 g/1 lb 2 oz mussels, cleaned and bearded
175 ml/6 fl oz water
100 ml/3^1/$_2$ fl oz dry white wine
1 tbsp lemon juice
4 tbsp olive oil
6 garlic cloves
20 whole blanched almonds
8 tbsp stale breadcrumbs
5 tbsp chopped flat-leafed parsley
^{1}/$_2$ tsp paprika
pinch of saffron threads
1^1/$_2$ tbsp flour
600 ml/1 pint Fish Stock (page 196)
600 g/1 lb 5 oz firm white fish, such as halibut, bass or
monkfish, cut into 4 cm/1^1/$_2$ inch chunks
2 small leeks, halved lengthways and thinly sliced
salt and freshly ground black pepper

Put the mussels in a large heavy-based saucepan with the water,
wine and lemon juice. Cook, tightly covered, over high heat
for 5 minutes until the shells open, shaking the pan occasionally. Strain the cooking liquid through a muslin-lined
sieve and reserve. Discard any mussels that have not opened.
Remove the rest from their shells and set them aside.

Heat the oil in a large saucepan or casserole. Add the
whole, peeled garlic and fry over medium heat until just

golden. Transfer to a blender using a perforated spoon. Fry the almonds in the same oil until just golden and add these to the garlic in the blender.

Fry the breadcrumbs until golden and add to the blender with 2 tablespoons of the parsley, the paprika, saffron, flour and about 4 tablespoons of the fish stock. Blend to a smooth paste, then gradually pour in the rest of the stock and process again.

Tip the contents of the blender back into the saucepan along with 150 ml/¼ pint of the mussel cooking liquid. Add the fish pieces and leeks. Simmer for 10–12 minutes then season with salt and pepper. Add the mussels and heat through. Check the seasoning and stir in the remaining parsley before serving.

Poultry Soups

Steaming hot, sweetly fragrant and easy on the digestion, the curative properties of chicken soup are universally acknowledged. There are infinite varieties of poultry soups to be enjoyed, made not only with chicken but with turkey, duck, goose and feathered game birds as well.

The recipes in this chapter sing with flavour and colour. They range from the deeply comforting classic chicken soup with matzo balls, to a rich and elegant creation with pheasant and red cabbage, and a vibrant Mexican-style soup of chargrilled chicken, tomato and lime. There is also a useful recipe for Christmas left-overs combining turkey, cranberries and Brazil nuts in a flavourful broth.

With the skin removed, poultry is relatively low in fat. It is also a valuable source of B vitamins and zinc.

THE RECIPES

COCKALEEKIE

SERVES 6

This is a real meal–in–a–plate, needing only good bread as an accompaniment. It is essential to use home-made stock. The prunes are a classic addition, providing a pleasant touch of sweetness, but can be left out if you prefer.

1.3 kg/3 lb chicken or chicken joints
2.5 litres/4¹/₂ pints Rich Meat Stock (page 190) or
Chicken Stock (page 188) or a mixture of both
4 large leeks, trimmed
fresh herb sprigs such as parsley, thyme, bay leaf and lovage,
tied in a bundle
50 g/1³/₄ oz pearl barley
¹/₂ tsp salt
150 g/5¹/₂ oz prunes
freshly ground black pepper
4 tbsp chopped parsley

Put the chicken in a large saucepan and cover with the stock. Bring to the boil slowly, skimming until the grey scum has gone. Tie half the leeks in a bundle and add to the pan with the herbs, pearl barley and salt. Simmer for 45 minutes with the lid askew until the chicken is almost cooked – if using chicken pieces, 30 minutes should be long enough.

While the chicken is cooking, separate the green and white parts of the remaining leeks. Cut the white part into diagonal slices. Finely chop the green part and set aside.

When the chicken is nearly cooked, fish out the whole leeks and herbs. Add the prunes and sliced leeks cook for another 20 minutes. Season with pepper, and more salt if necessary.

Remove the chicken and take the meat off the bone. Put the meat back into the soup, stir in the green leek and parsley, and serve.

Grilled Sweetcorn and Chilli Chowder (page 4),
with Chilli and Coriander Corn Muffins (page 210)

Roasted Squash, Chilli and Pumpkin Seed Soup (page 14)

ck and White Bean Soup with Red Pepper and Chorizo (page 52), with
Avocado and Chilli Sauce (page 227)

Chick-Pea and Grilled Aubergine Soup with Yogurt and Mint (page 5

Vietnamese Noodle Soup with Chicken and Oriental Greens (page 96)

Callaloo with Prawns (page 114), with Lime-Thyme Cream (page 232)

Cockaleekie (page 126)

Lamb, Courgette and Sweetcorn Soup with Mint (page 162)

CHICKEN SOUP WITH
MATZO BALLS

This is a classic comforter – no freezer should be
without it. It is essential to use good home-made stock.
You can use the chicken meat from stock-making in
the soup. For a really hefty meal, serve with Piroshkis
(page 202) or Filo Triangles (page 205). However, the
soup is filling enough on its own.

600 g/1 lb 5 oz skinless, boneless chicken, cut into chunks
1.3 litres/2 1/4 pints Chicken Stock (page 188) or Rich Meat
Stock (page 190)
2 carrots, sliced
1 leek, sliced
1 onion, chopped
2 celery stalks, sliced
2 garlic cloves, peeled but kept whole
salt and freshly ground black pepper
50 g/1 3/4 oz vermicelli
Matzo Balls (page 219)
3 tbsp chopped fresh parsley

Put the chicken meat in a large saucepan with the stock.
Slowly bring to the boil, skimming off any scum. Add the
vegetables, cover and simmer for 30–40 minutes. Season
with salt and pepper.

Add the vermicelli and cook for 5 minutes until just
tender. Raise the heat a bit so the soup is bubbling, then
drop in the matzo balls. Cover and cook for 10 minutes. Stir
in the parsley before serving.

GRILLED CHICKEN, TOMATO AND LIME SOUP

SERVES 4–5

This is a great soup with really zingy flavours. All the
vegetables are grilled, rather than fried, before they are
turned into a soup. If you don't have a stove-top grill pan,
use an ordinary grill pan set under a preheated very hot
grill 10–13 cm/4–5 inches from the heat source.
Serve with Avocado and Chilli Sauce (page 227) or
diced avocado tossed in lime juice, and warmed tortillas.
If you're really hungry, serve with Black Bean Salsa
(page 228) as well.

650 g/1 lb 7 oz boneless, skinless chicken breasts
oil for brushing
1 red or white onion, sliced horizontally into thick rings
500 g/1 lb 2 oz tomatoes, halved horizontally
1 fleshy green chilli
5 large garlic cloves, unpeeled
850 ml/1 1/2 pints Chicken Stock (page 188)
10 coriander sprigs, tied in a bunch
salt and freshly ground black pepper
2 tbsp lime juice

TO GARNISH
coriander sprigs
lime wedges

Halve the chicken breasts horizontally and brush with oil.
Place on a preheated ridged stove-top grill pan. Cook for 3
minutes each side, until the chicken is beginning to blacken
slightly but is still juicy inside. Cut into thin strips and set
aside.

Lightly brush the onion rings with oil. Grill with the tomatoes for about 7–10 minutes, turning, until slightly blackened. Then grill the chilli and garlic for 10 minutes.

Roughly chop the tomatoes and onion. Remove the skin and seeds from the chilli and chop the flesh. Peel and chop the garlic. Put all the vegetables in a saucepan with the stock, coriander, and salt and pepper. Bring to the boil then simmer gently for 20 minutes. Remove the coriander.

Add the chicken to the soup. Simmer for a few minutes more until heated through. Add the lime juice and check the seasoning.

Pour into bowls and garnish with coriander sprigs and lime wedges.

CHICKEN AND CHICK-PEA SOUP WITH ROASTED CHILLI CREAM

SERVES 4

Chick-peas give a lovely earthy flavour to this substantial warming soup. Together with chicken, they provide plenty of B vitamins as well as calcium, magnesium, iron and zinc. Serve the soup with warmed tortillas.

200 g/7 oz chick-peas, soaked overnight
2 tbsp olive oil
2 boneless, skinless chicken breasts, weighing
about 115 g/4 oz each, thickly sliced
1 onion, finely chopped
3 tender celery stalks with leaves, thinly sliced
3 garlic cloves, finely chopped
1 fresh red or green chilli, deseeded and finely chopped
$^1/_2$ tsp dried oregano
200 g/7 oz can chopped tomatoes
1 tbsp tomato purée
salt and freshly ground black pepper
1 litre/1$^3/_4$ pints Chicken Stock (page 188) or
Vegetable Stock (page 180)
Roasted Chilli Cream (page 234)
chopped fresh coriander or flat-leafed parsley, to garnish

Drain the chick-peas and put in a saucepan with plenty of fresh water to cover. Bring to the boil and boil rapidly for 15 minutes. Reduce the heat to a brisk simmer and continue to cook for about another 25–35 minutes until tender. Drain and set aside.

Heat the oil in a large saucepan. Add the chicken and fry over medium heat until lightly browned. Remove from the pan and cut into shreds.

Add the onion and celery to the pan, cover and gently fry until soft but not coloured. Stir in the garlic, chilli and oregano and fry for another minute. Add the chick-peas, tomatoes and tomato purée, and season with salt and pepper.

Pour in the stock, bring to the boil, then cover and simmer gently for 30 minutes or until the chick-peas are soft. Purée about one-third of the mixture and return to the pan. Add the chicken and check the seasoning. Cook for 5 minutes more.

Ladle into bowls, swirl in the roasted chilli cream and sprinkle with chopped coriander or parsley.

GRILLED CHICKEN AND SPINACH SOUP WITH COCONUT, LIME AND GINGER

SERVES 4

This is a thinnish soup with an oriental flavour and lovely textures – crisp water chestnuts and velvety spinach. Served with plainly boiled jasmine rice or thin egg noodles, or some Omelette Chunks (page 213), it makes an excellent light lunch or late-night supper.

600 g / 1 lb 5 oz boneless, skinless chicken breasts
oil for brushing
3 stalks lemon grass
1 lime
400 g / 14 oz can coconut milk
600 ml / 1 pint Chicken Stock (page 188) or
Chinese Stock (page 189)
4 spring onions, green parts included, sliced diagonally
2.5 cm / 1 inch piece fresh ginger root, grated
2 large fresh red chillies, deseeded and finely sliced
8 canned water chestnuts, sliced horizontally
¹/₂ tbsp light soy sauce
salt and freshly ground black pepper
115 g / 4 oz baby spinach, roughly chopped
1 tbsp cornflour mixed with 2 tbsp cold water

Halve the chicken breasts horizontally and brush with oil. Place on a preheated ridged cast-iron stove-top grill pan. Cook for 3 minutes each side, until the chicken is beginning to blacken slightly but is still juicy inside. Cut into thin strips and set aside.

Remove the tough outer leaves from the lemon grass, and bruise the inner stalks. Peel the rind from the lime, keeping it in large strips, taking care not to include the bitter white pith. Cut the lime in half and squeeze the juice.

Pour the coconut milk and stock into a large saucepan. Add the lemon grass, lime rind and juice, spring onions, ginger and chillies. Slowly bring to the boil, reduce the heat and simmer for 10 minutes. Discard the lemon grass and lime rind.

Bring back to a gentle boil and add the water chestnuts, chicken, soy sauce, and salt and pepper. Simmer for 4–5 minutes until the chicken is heated through.

Add the spinach and cook for a few seconds until just wilted. Stir in the cornflour paste, cook gently until slightly thickened and serve.

CHICKEN GUMBO

SERVES 6

This is a main–meal Cajun classic – thick and hearty and packed with flavour. Serve it with plainly boiled white rice to soak up the rich juices.

225 g/8 oz andouille sausage or chorizo, thickly sliced
1.3 kg/3 lb chicken thighs
seasoned flour for dredging
groundnut oil
1 onion, finely chopped
1 celery stalk, thinly sliced
1 green pepper, halved, deseeded and cut
into 1 cm/^{1}/$_2$ inch squares
3 garlic cloves, very finely chopped
1 tbsp plain flour
1 tsp hot pepper sauce, such as Tabasco or Pick-a-Pepper
200 g/7 oz can chopped tomatoes
350 g/12 oz okra, trimmed and halved lengthways
115 g/4 oz fresh or frozen sweetcorn kernels
1.2 litres/2 pints Chicken Stock (page 188)
salt and freshly ground black pepper

Fry the sausage in a large heavy-based saucepan or casserole over medium heat until browned and the fat starts to run. Remove with a perforated spoon and set aside.

Dredge the chicken joints in the seasoned flour and add to the pan, in batches if necessary. Add a little oil if you need to. Cook until evenly browned on the outside but still juicy on the inside. Remove and set aside.

Drain off all but 2 tablespoons of oil. Add the onion, celery, green pepper and garlic. Cook over medium-low heat until soft. Stir in the flour and cook for 1 minute.

Add the hot pepper sauce, tomatoes and okra. Cover and

cook for 15 minutes. Then add the corn and cook for another minute. Gradually pour in the stock, stirring, and bring to a gentle boil.

Remove the chicken meat from the bones and add to the soup along with the sausage. Season with salt and pepper. Lower the heat and cook for 15 minutes. Check the seasoning before serving.

MOROCCAN CHICKEN HARIRA

SERVES 6–8

This soup is served to break the fast every evening
during the month of Ramadan. It is extremely rich
and nourishing. Serve it with pitta bread or, more
authentically, with dates and figs. Harissa sauce is
a fiery thick red sauce used as a condiment.
You can buy it in large supermarkets and
Middle Eastern food stores.

1 chicken weighing about 1.3–1.5 kg/3 lb–3 lb 5 oz
2 tbsp olive oil
1 onion, coarsely chopped
¹/₂ tsp ground turmeric
¹/₂ tsp freshly ground black pepper
¹/₂ tsp ground ginger
¹/₂ tsp ground cinnamon
¹/₄ tsp saffron threads ground with 1 tsp salt
150 g/5¹/₂ oz chick-peas, soaked overnight and drained
4 large tomatoes, peeled and chopped
1.5 litres/2 ³/₄ pints water
150 g/5¹/₂ oz long-grain rice, rinsed
2 tbsp flour
juice of 1 lemon
6 tbsp chopped fresh coriander
6 tbsp chopped fresh flat-leafed parsley
lemon wedges, to garnish
harissa sauce, to serve

Cut the legs and breast portions, including the wings, off the
chicken and split the carcass in two. Heat the oil in a large
non-stick frying pan and fry the chicken pieces on all sides.
Transfer to a large saucepan or casserole.

Gently fry the onion in the oil remaining in the frying

pan. When soft, stir in the spices, sizzle for a few seconds, then add the drained chick-peas and tomatoes. Heat through, then add to the chicken along with 1.4 litres/2½ pints of the water. Bring to the boil, then cover and simmer gently for about 45 minutes until the chick-peas are tender.

Using a perforated spoon, remove the chicken from the pan and discard the skin and bones. Blot the fat from the surface of the soup with paper towels. Return the meat to the pan and add the rice. Bring to the boil, then reduce the heat and simmer gently for another 15–20 minutes until the rice is cooked.

Meanwhile, put the flour in a small saucepan and gradually beat in the remaining 100 ml/¼ pint of water. Add a bit of liquid from the hot soup and stir over a low heat until the mixture begins to boil. Pour into the soup along with the lemon juice and most of the coriander and parsley. Add more water if the mixture is too thick. Check the seasoning.

Pour into bowls and sprinkle with the rest of the coriander and parsley. Garnish with lemon wedges and serve with a small bowl of harissa sauce.

CHICKEN, PEA AND SWEETCORN SOUP WITH MINT

SERVES 4–5

I love to serve this soup in early summer when the first of the peas and mint are making an appearance. However, the soup is nearly as good (and very quick) made with frozen peas and sweetcorn, so you can use it to brighten up a winter's day as well. It is delicious with a dish of buttery new potatoes.

2 tbsp sunflower or safflower oil
450 g/1 lb boneless, skinless chicken, cut into
2 cm/³/₄ inch pieces
2 shallots, finely chopped
2 tbsp chopped fresh mint
2–3 potatoes, diced
150 g/5¹/₂ oz fresh or frozen shelled peas
150 g/5¹/₂ oz fresh or frozen sweetcorn kernels
salt and freshly ground black pepper
850 ml/1¹/₂ pints Chicken Stock (page 188)
squeeze of lemon juice
soured cream
mint sprigs, to garnish

Heat the oil in a large saucepan and fry the chicken over medium-high heat until beginning to brown. Remove from the pan with a perforated spoon and set aside.

Add the shallots, mint and potatoes to the pan. Cover and cook over medium-low heat for 5 minutes. Add the peas and sweetcorn and cook for 2 minutes more. Season to taste with salt and pepper. Pour in the stock, bring to the boil, then simmer for 5 minutes.

Leave about one-third of the vegetables in the pan and

purée the rest in a food processor or blender. Pour the purée back into the pan and add the chicken. Bring back to the boil, then simmer for a few minutes until the chicken is heated through. Add a squeeze of lemon juice to brighten the flavour, and check the seasoning.

Garnish each bowl with a swirl of soured cream and a mint sprig.

GREEN TURKEY SOUP

SERVES 4

This soup can also be made with chicken breasts, pork
fillet or even left-over Christmas turkey. Full of bright
Mexican flavours, it makes a welcome change after the
Christmas festivities. The soup is rich in beta-carotene
and low in fat.

1 yellow pepper
2 green peppers
3 fleshy green chillies
2 garlic cloves, unpeeled
500 g/1 lb 2 oz turkey fillets
3 tbsp olive oil
$^{1}/_{2}$ tsp cumin seeds
1 tsp coriander seeds
$^{1}/_{2}$ tsp dried oregano
50 g/1$^{3}/_{4}$ oz chopped white onion
25 g/1 oz trimmed, chopped fresh coriander
4 cos lettuce leaves without stalks, shredded
1 small corn tortilla, cut into strips
juice of 1 lime
600 ml/1 pint Chicken Stock (page 188)
warmed taco shells, crumbled
crème fraîche, to garnish

Preheat the oven to 220°C (210°C fan oven)/gas 7.
Roast the peppers for 10 minutes, then add the chillies
and garlic and roast for another 10 minutes until the
pepper and chilli skins blister and blacken and the garlic
is soft. Set aside the yellow pepper. When cool enough
to handle, remove the skins and seeds from the chillies
and remaining peppers, and the skin from the garlic.
Roughly chop the flesh.

Brush the turkey fillets with a little of the oil. Place on a preheated ridged cast-iron stove-top grill pan. Cook for 3 minutes each side, until beginning to blacken slightly but still juicy inside. Cut into bite-sized strips and set aside.

Dry-fry the cumin and coriander seeds in a small heavy-based pan until you can smell the aroma. Add the oregano and fry for a few seconds. Immediately remove from the pan. Crush to a powder with a pestle and mortar.

Put the peppers, chillies and garlic in a blender with the dry-fried seed mixture and the onion, coriander, lettuce, tortilla and lime juice. Purée until smooth, adding a bit of stock or water if necessary.

Heat the remaining oil in a large saucepan. Add the purée and fry over medium-high heat for 2–3 minutes. Pour in the stock and bring to a gentle boil. Add the turkey and simmer for 10 minutes to blend the flavours.

Peel the reserved pepper, remove the seeds and cut the flesh into neat squares.

Ladle the soup into bowls and sprinkle with the yellow pepper and crumbled taco shells. Stir in a blob of crème fraîche.

LEFT-OVER TURKEY SOUP WITH CRANBERRIES AND BRAZIL NUTS

SERVES 4–5

This is a wonderful soup for using up Christmas left-overs, and it works just as well made with goose or duck. Brazil nuts are incredibly rich in selenium, an important trace mineral thought to protect against cancer. Just two nuts a day provide well over the recommended daily allowance.

1 tbsp sunflower or safflower oil
1 small red onion, finely chopped
2 tender celery stalks, finely sliced
2 small carrots, coarsely grated
4 spring onions, green parts included, thinly sliced
50 g/1³/₄ oz dried cranberries
1 plum tomato, peeled, deseeded and chopped
salt and freshly ground black pepper
1 litre/1³/₄ pints Chicken Stock (page 188) or
Game Bird Stock (page 194)
450 g/1 lb boneless, skinless cooked turkey, cubed
115 g/4 oz cooked wild rice or basmati rice, or a mixture
2 tsp balsamic vinegar
3 tbsp chopped fresh parsley
40 g/1¹/₂ oz Brazil nuts, coarsely chopped

Heat the oil in a large saucepan. Add the onion and celery, cover and cook over medium–low heat for 5 minutes. Add the carrots, spring onions, cranberries and tomato and cook for a minute or two more until tender but still brightly coloured. Season with salt and a generous grinding of black pepper.

Pour in the stock, bring to the boil and add the turkey. Reduce the heat and simmer, uncovered, for 10 minutes until the turkey is heated through. Stir in the rice, vinegar and parsley, and check the seasoning. Ladle into bowls, sprinkle with the nuts and serve.

PHEASANT, PANCETTA AND RED CABBAGE SOUP

SERVES 6–8

Red cabbage usually becomes disappointingly tasteless when cooked in a soup, but here it combines well with pheasant, pancetta and earthy Puy lentils. The soup is delicious served with Grilled Polenta (page 212) and a green salad.

115 g/4 oz pancetta or streaky bacon, diced
2 tbsp olive oil
2 small pheasants, weighing about 1.3 kg/3 lb in total, jointed
salt and freshly ground black pepper
2 leeks, finely sliced
2 carrots, sliced
1 celery stalk, finely sliced
280 g/10 oz shredded red cabbage
400 g/14 oz can chopped tomatoes
1 fresh bay leaf
2–3 thyme sprigs
100 ml/3^1/$_2$ fl oz red wine
2 litres/3^1/$_2$ pints Game Bird Stock (page 194) or Chicken Stock (page 188)
115 g/4 oz Puy lentils
2 tsp balsamic vinegar
chopped flat-leafed parsley, to garnish

Brown the pancetta or bacon in a large heavy-based saucepan or casserole until crisp. Remove with a perforated spoon, drain on paper towels and set aside to use later as a garnish.

Heat the oil in the same pan, and lightly brown the pheasant joints over medium heat, seasoning with salt and pepper. Remove and set aside.

Add the leeks and gently fry for 5 minutes until just coloured. Add the carrots, celery and cabbage. Cover and cook for 5 minutes until softened. Stir in the tomatoes, bay leaf, thyme, and season with salt and pepper.

Return the pheasant pieces to the pan. Pour in the wine and stock and slowly bring to the boil, removing any scum. Simmer gently with the lid askew for 30 minutes. Add the lentils and simmer for another 45 minutes until the pheasant and lentils are tender.

Fish out the pheasant pieces, bay leaf and thyme. Strip the meat, discarding the skin and bones. Return the meat to the pan, and reheat gently. Add the vinegar, and, if necessary, more salt and pepper.

Ladle the soup into bowls and garnish with the reserved pancetta and a sprinkling of parsley.

PRESERVED DUCK OR GOOSE SOUP

SERVES 8

If you brought back cans of preserved goose or duck from holidays in France and then wondered what to do with them, this is the soup for you. It is wonderfully rich and satisfying, and makes an impressive winter Saturday lunch when you have guests. Serve it with a big green salad and some good cheese.

225 g/8 oz dried haricot beans, soaked overnight
8 pieces preserved goose or duck, halved if large
1 onion, chopped
3 carrots, diced
2 turnips, diced
1 leek, sliced
2 garlic cloves, finely chopped
fresh bouquet garni of 2–3 thyme sprigs, 6 parsley sprigs,
celery leaf, bay leaf, tied with string
$1/2$ tsp cayenne pepper
1 tsp salt
freshly ground black pepper
2 litres/3$1/2$ pints Chicken Stock (page 188)
2 potatoes, cubed
1 small dark green cabbage, quartered, cored, tough
stalks removed
slices of stale French bread

Drain the haricot beans and put in a saucepan with plenty of water to cover. Bring to the boil, boil rapidly for 15 minutes then cook for another 30–45 minutes until tender but not breaking up. Drain again.

Drain the preserved goose or duck from its fat; set the

meat aside. Heat 3 tablespoons of the fat in a large saucepan or casserole. Add the onion, carrots, turnips, leek and garlic and cook gently for 20 minutes until soft. Add the bouquet garni, cayenne, salt and pepper.

Pour in the stock, bring to the boil then add the haricot beans, potatoes and cabbage. Simmer very gently for 30 minutes, stirring occasionally.

Bury the pieces of goose or duck in the soup and cook for another 30 minutes, removing any scum that floats to the surface. Remove the bouquet garni.

Place some stale bread in the base of individual soup bowls and ladle the soup over, making sure everyone gets some of the goose or duck.

Meat and Game Soups

Meat and game make the heartiest of main meal soups and, combined with vegetables and grains or pulses, are among the most nutritionally well balanced. Meat is a major source of B vitamins and protein. Red meat in particular provides valuable iron, often under-supplied in the Western diet. The actual amount of meat served in a soup is naturally small so the drawbacks of cholesterol and saturated fat are kept to a minimum, particularly if visible fat is removed. Fat is not an issue with game meat such as venison and rabbit, since both contain minuscule amounts.

This chapter features excellent meat soups from countries as far-ranging as Mexico, Hungary and Wales, as well as a few of my own inventions. These seriously big soups will have you staggering from the table.

THE RECIPES

MEXICAN BEEF, CHILLI AND VEGETABLE SOUP

SERVES 8

This is a big beefy soup inspired by a recipe from the excellent *Food From My Heart* by Zarela Martínez. The vegetables are cooked separately, so that they keep their shape and colour, and added to the meat and broth at the last minute. Dried chillies are available from healthfood shops and speciality food shops. Epazote is a Mexican herb that is easy to grow but not to buy. Thyme is a reasonable substitute. The soup needs hunks of bread for mopping up juices and perhaps some grated Cheddar cheese to sprinkle on top.

450 g/1 lb large flavourful tomatoes
5 dried Anaheim or guajillo chillies
2 dried ancho or mulato chillies
1 small onion, cut into wedges
2 garlic cloves, peeled but kept whole
1 tbsp dried oregano
2 tbsp olive oil
1.1 kg/2 lb 8 oz shin of beef, cubed
2–3 veal bones, cracked
handful of epazote sprigs (see page 240) or thyme sprigs
salt and freshly ground black pepper
6 new potatoes
2–3 carrots, quartered lengthways and cut into
2.5 cm/1 inch pieces
350 g/12 oz green beans, cut into 2.5 cm/1 inch pieces
2 courgettes, halved lengthways and thickly sliced
150 g/5 oz fresh or frozen sweetcorn kernels
6 tbsp chopped fresh coriander

Place the tomatoes in a grill pan or on a preheated ridged cast-iron stove-top grill pan. Grill, turning, until blackened. Put in a bowl to catch the juices, and set aside.

Remove the seeds, stalk and any veins from the dried chillies. Grill, turning, for no more than 10–20 seconds until you smell the aroma (be very careful not to let them burn). Place in a bowl and just cover with hot but not boiling water. Leave to soak for 20 minutes, then drain.

Put the tomatoes, including any blackened skin, in a blender with the chillies, onion, garlic and oregano. Purée, adding a bit of water if necessary, then push through a sieve.

Heat the oil in a large saucepan or casserole. Brown the meat and bones, then add the chilli purée and cook, stirring, for 2–3 minutes. Add the epazote or thyme and enough water to cover. Season with salt and pepper. Bring to the boil then reduce the heat and simmer gently with the lid askew for 1½–2 hours until the meat is tender. Remove the bones and blot up any fat with paper towel.

While the meat is cooking, cook the potatoes, carrots and beans in a steamer set over boiling water – or plunge them separately into a large pan of boiling water – until just tender. Remove from the heat as soon as they are cooked, and drain under cold running water. Cut the potatoes into quarters.

About 10 minutes before you're ready to serve the soup, add the cooked vegetables, the courgettes and sweetcorn. Bring to the boil then simmer for 5 minutes until the courgettes and sweetcorn are just cooked. Check the seasoning, stir in the coriander and serve.

PORK, BEANS AND GREENS SOUP WITH CORIANDER AND LIME

SERVES 8

This is a great main meal soup for a casual weekend
dinner with friends. If you can't get *cavalo nero*
(an Italian cabbage with dark crinkly leaves), use Savoy
cabbage or kale. Leafy greens such as these contain
extremely high levels of beta-carotene, an antioxidant
strongly implicated in protection against cancer.
Leafy greens are also a good source of essential minerals
such as iron and zinc. Serve the soup with Chilli and
Coriander Corn Muffins (page 210), tortillas or tostadas
(crisp fried corn tortillas).

200 g/7 oz appaloosa beans, borlotti beans or red kidney beans,
soaked overnight
4 tbsp groundnut oil
600 g/1 lb 5 oz lean boneless pork, cut into 2 cm/^{3}/$_4$ inch cubes
3 white onions, thinly sliced
1 tsp cumin seeds, crushed
^{1}/$_2$ tsp dried thyme or oregano
3 large garlic cloves, very finely chopped
1–3 jalapeño chillies, deseeded and finely chopped
3 large tomatoes, peeled and chopped
1.5 litres/2^3/$_4$ pints Chinese Stock (page 189) or
Chicken Stock (page 188)
^{1}/$_2$ tsp salt
^{1}/$_2$ tsp freshly ground black pepper
550 g/1 lb 4 oz cavalo nero, tough stalks removed, leaves
finely shredded (about 175 g/6 oz trimmed cabbage)
8 tbsp chopped fresh coriander
2–3 tbsp lime juice

TO GARNISH
thinly sliced white onion
diced avocado
lime wedges

Drain the beans and put in a saucepan with fresh water to cover. Bring to the boil, boil rapidly for 15 minutes, then cook at a brisk simmer for another 30–45 minutes until soft. Drain and set aside.

Heat the oil in a large saucepan or casserole over medium-high heat. Add the pork and fry until lightly browned. Remove from the pan with a perforated spoon and set aside.

Reduce the heat to low and add the onion, cumin and oregano, stirring to coat in the fat. Cover and gently fry for 25–30 minutes, stirring occasionally, until very soft. Then add the garlic, chilli and tomatoes and their juices. Cover and fry for 10 minutes.

When the mixture is very soft, add the meat, beans, stock and the salt and pepper. Bring to the boil, then reduce the heat and simmer gently, with the lid slightly askew, for 45 minutes until the meat is tender.

Raise the heat to a brisk simmer and stir in the cabbage. Cover and simmer for 10 minutes more until the cabbage is tender.

Stir in the coriander and lime juice just before serving. Serve the garnishes in small bowls from which people can help themselves.

HAM AND ROOT SOUP

SERVES 6

A hearty soup, perfect for a winter weekend lunch when you have a houseful of guests. Use a mixture of whatever roots you have to hand – parsnips, celeriac, potatoes, swedes or whatever. Roots are rich in slow-release carbohydrate to keep your energy levels up. Serve with big hunks of farmhouse bread.

2 tbsp sunflower or grapeseed oil
1 fresh bay leaf, torn
1 tsp chopped fresh rosemary
200 g/7 oz chunk of good ham, diced
1 large onion, finely chopped
2 celery stalks, halved lengthways, then sliced crossways
800 g/1 lb 12 oz peeled and trimmed mixed
root vegetables, diced
1 litre/1³⁄₄ pints Ham Hock Stock (page 191),
Chicken Stock (page 188) or Vegetable Stock (page 180)
salt and freshly ground black pepper
snipped fresh chives, to garnish

Heat the oil with the bay leaf and rosemary in a large pan over medium heat. Add the ham and stir-fry for a few minutes until beginning to crisp round the edges. Remove the ham with a perforated spoon and set aside.

Add the onion and celery, cover and leave to cook over medium-low heat for about 5 minutes. When nicely softened, tip in the roots, stir everything around, then cover and cook over gentle heat for another 10 minutes.

Pour in the stock and bring to the boil, then reduce the heat and simmer, partially covered, for 30 minutes.

Purée about half the mixture – depending on how chunky you like your soup – until smooth. Pour this back into the saucepan and stir in the ham. Cook over gentle heat until heated through. Season with a little salt, remembering the saltiness of the ham, and plenty of freshly ground black pepper. Sprinkle with chives before serving.

GOULASH SOUP WITH CSIPETKE

SERVES 4–6

Csipetke are little 'pinched' dumplings – a favourite
addition to this richly flavoured Hungarian soup.
If you don't feel up to making these, you could bulk
the soup up with 350 g/12 oz cubed potatoes instead –
add them to the soup with the pepper and tomatoes – or
use Herb or Lemon Pepper Dumplings (page 220).
Blinis (page 201) topped with a dollop of smetana
or soured cream, or some Mushroom, Dill and
Lemon Stuffed Leaves (page 216) would be
delicious accompaniments.

1 tbsp safflower or sunflower oil
1 large onion, chopped
2 tsp paprika
$^1/_2$ tsp caraway seeds
pinch of chilli powder
2 garlic cloves, crushed
1 tbsp tomato purée mixed with 1 tbsp water
550 g/1 lb 4 oz shin of beef, cut into 1 cm/$^1/_2$ inch chunks
1 green pepper, halved, deseeded and finely diced
2 tomatoes, peeled and finely diced
850 ml/1$^1/_2$ pints Rich Meat Stock (page 190)
salt and freshly ground black pepper

FOR THE CSIPETKE DOUGH
75 g/2$^3/_4$ oz plain flour
$^1/_2$ tsp salt
1 egg, lightly beaten

TO SERVE
soured cream mixed with chopped fresh dill

Heat the oil in a large saucepan. Add the onion and fry over medium heat until golden. Stir in the paprika, caraway seeds, chilli powder, garlic and diluted tomato purée.

Next, add the beef and fry until browned. Cover tightly and simmer over the lowest possible heat for 1 hour, adding a ladleful of the stock if the mixture becomes too dry.

Meanwhile, make the *csipetke* dough. Sift the flour and salt into a bowl. Make a well in the middle and pour in the egg. Mix with a fork, gradually drawing in the flour from around the edge. Knead vigorously for 10 minutes until silky smooth and springy. Cover with clingfilm and leave to rest for 30 minutes.

Add the green pepper and tomato to the soup. Cover and cook for 5 minutes. Then add the stock and simmer for 20 minutes more. Season with salt and pepper to taste.

Fifteen minutes before serving, roll out the dough and pinch off small pieces with your finger and thumb. Drop them into the simmering soup and cook for about 10 minutes. Serve the soup with a bowl of soured cream mixed with a little chopped dill.

BORSCH

SERVES 6

This classic Russian soup has countless variations, but it always contains beetroot and soured cream. This version made with meat and chunky vegetables comes from Moscow. Serve with Lemon Pepper or Herb Dumplings (page 220), or just some hunks of dark rye bread. If you're including the dumplings, precook them in water and add them to the soup at the end of cooking.

350 g/12 oz shin of beef
1 onion
1 turnip
1 carrot
450 g/1 lb uncooked beetroot
2 tbsp grapeseed or sunflower oil
1 tbsp tomato purée
2 tbsp red wine vinegar
$^1/_2$ tsp sugar
$^1/_2$ tsp salt
1.2 litres/2 pints Rich Meat Stock (page 190)
115 g/4 oz shredded cabbage
2 tbsp chopped fresh dill
1 tbsp chopped fresh lovage
2 tbsp chopped fresh parsley
2 garlic cloves, crushed with
$^1/_2$ tsp freshly ground black pepper
115 g/4 oz potatoes, diced
soured cream
chopped fresh dill or lovage, to garnish

Cut the meat and the vegetables into evenly sized dice – about 2 cm/³/₄ inch square.

Heat the oil in a large saucepan. Add the meat and fry for 10 minutes until browned. Add the onion, turnip and carrot, and gently fry for 5–7 minutes until softened. Then add the beetroot and cook for a few minutes more.

Stir in the tomato purée, vinegar, sugar, salt and 300 ml/½ pint of the stock. Cover and simmer very gently for 45 minutes.

Next add the cabbage, herbs and remaining stock. Cover and simmer for another 20 minutes, adding more salt or vinegar if you think it necessary.

Add the garlic and pepper mixture, and the potatoes. Cook for 10 minutes until the potatoes are soft. Remove from the heat, cover and leave to stand for 10 minutes.

Purée about one-third of the mixture in a food processor or blender until smooth. Return to the pan and mix with the rest of the soup. Add the dumplings, if using, and reheat gently.

Put a spoonful of soured cream in the bottom of each serving bowl and pour the soup over. Garnish with dill or lovage, and serve at once.

SCOTCH BROTH

SERVES 6–8

Another classic main meal soup, delicious served with
a big dish of floury boiled potatoes or some really good
white farmhouse bread.

6 lamb shanks, weighing about 1.6 kg/3¹/₂ lb
2 large onions
1 head of garlic
1 tbsp safflower or sunflower oil
4 rashers unsmoked bacon, derinded and diced
3 carrots, sliced
1 small swede, cut into chunks
1 small celeriac, cut into chunks
3 leeks, halved lengthways and thickly sliced
2 thyme sprigs
1 fresh bay leaf
700 ml/1¹/₄ pint Lamb Stock (page 192),
Chicken Stock (page 188) or water
50 g/1³/₄ oz pearl barley
1 tsp salt
1 tsp freshly ground black pepper
4 tbsp chopped fresh parsley

Preheat the oven to 230°C (220°C fan oven)/gas 7. Put the
lamb shanks in a roasting tin. Cut one of the onions into
quarters. Remove the outer layers of loose papery skin from
the garlic and slice the head in half horizontally. Put the
onion quarters and garlic halves in the pan with the meat.
Roast in the preheated oven for 30 minutes, turning the
meat now and then, until everything is brown and roasted.

Transfer the lamb, onion and garlic to a large saucepan
with enough water to cover. Bring to the boil very slowly,
skimming any foam from the surface. Reduce the heat to

the barest simmer and cook with the lid askew for about 1¼ hours until the meat is very tender.

Meanwhile, heat the oil in a large saucepan. Add the bacon and cook until crisp. Finely dice the remaining onion and add to the pan with the carrots, swede, celeriac, leeks, thyme and bay leaf. Pour in the stock and add the barley and the salt and pepper. Bring to the boil then reduce the heat and simmer gently for 30–35 minutes until the barley is tender. Remove from the heat and set aside.

When the lamb is cooked, lift the meat and garlic from the pan with a perforated spoon. Strip the meat from the bones, discarding fat and gristle. Squeeze the pulp from the garlic and set aside.

Strain the liquid through a muslin-lined sieve into a bowl. Blot up the fat with paper towels. Add 750 ml/1¼ pints of this liquid to the vegetables along with the meat and the garlic pulp. Bring back to the boil, then simmer for 10 minutes. Check the seasoning. Stir in the parsley just before serving.

LAMB, COURGETTE AND SWEETCORN SOUP WITH MINT

Soups made with lamb tend to be of the Scotch Broth variety with traditional flavours. Here is one with a bit more zing – provided by cumin, chilli, lemon juice and mint. Serve with Chilli and Coriander Corn Muffins (page 210) or just some crusty bread.

2 tbsp sunflower or safflower oil
500 g/1 lb 2 oz boneless lamb, cut into 2 cm/³/₄ inch cubes
1 onion, finely diced
1 red pepper, halved, deseeded and finely diced
¹/₂ tsp cumin seeds, crushed
¹/₂ tsp dried oregano
¹/₂ tsp dried chilli flakes
2 garlic cloves, very finely chopped
4 tomatoes, peeled, deseeded and chopped
1 tbsp tomato purée
1 litre/1³/₄ pints Lamb Stock (page 192), or
Chicken Stock (page 188)
¹/₂ tsp salt
freshly ground black pepper
1–2 tbsp lemon juice
200 g/7 oz fresh or frozen sweetcorn kernels
3 small courgettes, diced
2 tbsp chopped fresh mint

Heat the oil in a large saucepan over medium–high heat. Add the lamb and fry until lightly browned. Remove and set aside.

Add the onion, red pepper, cumin seeds, oregano and chilli flakes to the pan. Reduce the heat a bit and gently fry for 5 minutes until softened. Then add the garlic, tomatoes and tomato purée, and cook for a few more minutes until slightly reduced.

Return the meat to the pan and pour in the stock. Bring to the boil, then reduce the heat to low. Cover and simmer for 1 hour until the meat is meltingly tender.

Stir in the salt, pepper, lemon juice to taste, sweetcorn and courgettes, and cook for 3–5 minutes until the vegetables are tender but still brightly coloured. Stir in the mint just before serving.

SPICY LAMB AND YOGURT SOUP WITH STUFFED CABBAGE LEAVES

SERVES 4

Use the Spiced Red Pepper and Couscous Stuffing or
the Spiced Nut Stuffing (page 217) for the cabbage leaves.
Before adding to the soup, gently reheat the stuffed leaves
in a microwave or steamer basket set over boiling water.
Serve with warm naan bread or parathas.

2 garlic cloves, chopped
seeds from 3 cardamom pods
2.5 cm/1 inch piece fresh ginger root, finely chopped
$^1/_4$ tsp cayenne pepper
1 tsp coriander seeds, crushed
1 large onion, diced
600 g/1 lb 5 oz lean lamb, cut into 2 cm/$^3/_4$ inch cubes
1 tbsp sunflower or safflower oil
25 g/1 oz butter
1 tbsp flour
6 tbsp Greek yogurt
1 litre/1$^3/_4$ pints Lamb Stock (page 192) or
Chicken Stock (page 188)
$^1/_2$ tsp salt
freshly ground black pepper
25 g/1 oz ground almonds
pinch of saffron threads
3 tbsp single cream
3 tbsp chopped fresh mint
Stuffed Cabbage Leaves (pages 216–18), to serve

Put the garlic, cardamom, ginger, cayenne, coriander seeds
and half the diced onion in a blender and purée to a paste.
Add a bit of water or stock if necessary.

Put the meat cubes in a bowl and rub the spice paste into them. Cover and leave to stand for at least 2 hours or overnight in the fridge.

Heat the oil and butter in a large saucepan over medium heat. Add the remaining onion and gently fry until soft. Add the meat and fry until browned and most of the liquid has evaporated.

Sprinkle in the flour and cook for 1 minute then gradually stir in the yogurt, a tablespoonful at a time. Slowly pour in the stock and bring to the boil, stirring constantly. Season with the salt and pepper, then cover and simmer for 30 minutes.

Stir the almonds, saffron and cream into the soup and simmer for 15 minutes more, stirring occasionally.

Place the warm stuffed cabbage leaves in individual shallow soup plates and pour the soup over. Stir the mint into the soup just before serving.

GAME AND LENTIL SOUP

SERVES 4

This richly flavoured soup is delicious served with some crisply fried flat cap mushrooms on the side.

1 tbsp olive oil
25 g / 1 oz butter
450 g / 1 lb boneless game meat, such as venison,
wild boar, rabbit or bison, cut into 2 cm / $^3/_4$ inch cubes
1 small red onion, finely sliced
2 celery stalks, finely sliced
1 carrot, finely diced
2 large tomatoes, peeled, deseeded and chopped
150 g / 5$^1/_2$ oz Puy lentils
1.4 litres / 2$^1/_2$ pints Rich Game Stock (page 195)
1 bay leaf
2–3 fresh thyme sprigs
6 juniper berries, crushed
salt and freshly ground black pepper
1 tbsp crab apple or redcurrant jelly
2 tsp balsamic vinegar
chopped chives or parsley, to garnish
Garlic Croûtons (page 209)

Heat the oil and butter in a large saucepan and brown the game meat over medium–high heat. Remove from the pan using a perforated spoon and set aside.

Reduce the heat a little, add the onion, celery and carrot, and gently fry in the remaining oil and butter until softened. Add the tomatoes and fry for a few minutes more.

Return the meat to the pan, add the lentils, stock, bay leaf, thyme and juniper berries. Bring to the boil, removing any scum that floats to the surface. Reduce the heat, cover and simmer gently for 30 minutes until the meat and lentils are tender. Fish out the bay leaf and thyme stalks. Season with salt and pepper. Stir in the jelly and vinegar, and cook for 5 minutes more.

Ladle into bowls and sprinkle with chives or parsley and the croûtons.

VENISON, BORLOTTI BEAN AND CHILLI SOUP

SERVES 4

This is a favourite winter soup – low in fat but filling and flavourful. Serve it with Grilled Polenta (page 212) or Garlic Croûtons (page 209).

200 g/7 oz borlotti beans, soaked overnight,
or 400 g/14 oz drained canned beans (about 1¹/₂ cans)
¹/₂ tsp cumin seeds
1 tsp coriander seeds
1 tsp dried oregano
500 g/1 lb 2 oz stewing venison,
cut into 2 cm/³/₄ inch cubes
2 tbsp groundnut oil
1 onion, finely chopped
1 red pepper, deseeded and cut into 1 cm/¹/₂ inch squares
2 garlic cloves, very finely chopped
2–3 fresh red chillies, deseeded and finely chopped,
or 1 tsp chilli powder
200 g/7 oz can chopped tomatoes
1 tbsp tomato purée
¹/₂ tsp sugar
¹/₂ tsp salt
freshly ground black pepper
1.3 litres/2¹/₄ pints Rich Game Stock (page 195)
or Rich Meat Stock (page 190)
3 tbsp chopped fresh coriander
soured cream, to serve

Drain the soaked beans and put in a saucepan with plenty of water to cover. Bring to the boil and boil rapidly for 15 minutes. Reduce the heat to a brisk simmer and continue to cook until the beans are tender – up to 1 hour depending on the age of the beans. Drain and set aside. If using canned beans, rinse them and set aside.

Put the cumin and coriander seeds in a small heavy-based pan without any oil, and dry-fry over medium heat until the seeds smell fragrant. Sprinkle in the oregano and fry for a few seconds more. Immediately remove from the pan. Lightly crush the mixture using a pestle and mortar and toss with the meat. Leave to stand for 30 minutes.

Heat half the oil in a large saucepan. Add the meat and fry over medium-high heat until browned and most of the liquid has evaporated. Remove from the pan.

Heat the remaining oil in the same saucepan. Add the onion and red pepper, cover and cook over medium-low heat for 5–7 minutes until soft. Add the garlic, chillies or chilli powder and fry for another minute or so.

Put the meat back in the pan with the drained beans, tomatoes, tomato purée, sugar, salt and pepper. Pour in the stock, bring to the boil, skimming if necessary, then simmer for 50–60 minutes until the meat is tender.

Check the seasoning and stir in the coriander. Ladle into bowls and swirl in a slick of soured cream.

VENISON SOUP WITH MUSHROOMS AND DRIED SOUR CHERRIES

SERVES 4

This is a lovely combination of flavours – rich game and mushrooms lightened by the sweet sharpness of the cherries. You can buy dried sour cherries in good supermarkets. They are sometimes called Montmorency cherries. Serve with Garlic Croûtons (page 209) or Grilled Polenta (page 212).

2 tbsp plain flour
$^1/_2$ tsp salt
$^1/_2$ tsp freshly ground black pepper
500 g/1 lb 2 oz stewing venison, cut into 2 cm/$^3/_4$ inch dice
2 tbsp olive oil
25 g/1 oz butter
1 red onion, thinly sliced
2 carrots, thinly sliced
115 g/4 oz mushrooms, cut into small segments
2 garlic cloves, very finely chopped
50 g/1$^3/_4$ oz dried sour cherries
1.3 litres/2$^1/_4$ pints Rich Game Stock (page 195)
or Rich Meat Stock (page 190)

Combine the flour, salt and pepper. Pat the meat dry with paper towels and toss with the flour mixture until evenly coated. Don't do this until you're ready to cook, otherwise the flour becomes soggy.

Heat 1 tablespoon of the oil and the butter in a large saucepan over medium-high heat. When very hot, add the meat and sear on all sides. Remove from the pan and set aside.

Reduce the heat and add the remaining oil to the pan along with the onion. Cover and cook for 5 minutes until soft. Then add the carrots, mushrooms and garlic, and cook for a few minutes more.

Return the meat to the pan with the cherries. Pour in the stock and bring to the boil, skimming if necessary, then simmer for 50–60 minutes until the meat is tender. Check the seasoning before serving.

ROASTED RABBIT AND ROOT VEGETABLE SOUP

SERVES 6

Farmed rabbit is becoming more widely available and it is worth making the most of it. The meat is low in fat and has a distinctive but mild flavour. Combined with roasted root vegetables and pasta shapes, it makes a hearty soup. Serve with Bruschetta (page 207), Cheese Toasts (page 206) or crusty bread.

2 rabbits, jointed
1 tsp salt
freshly ground black pepper
3 tbsp chopped fresh rosemary
olive oil
2 carrots, cut into 2.5 cm/1 inch pieces
2 parsnips, cut into 2.5 cm/1 inch pieces
8 baby onions, peeled and left whole
3 fat garlic cloves, unpeeled
115 g/4 oz very small pasta shapes, such as orzi, farfalline
or ditali rigati
1.3 litres/2¼ pints Chicken Stock (page 188)
85 g/3 oz thinly shredded green cabbage

Preheat the oven to 200°C (190°C fan oven)/gas 6. Pat the rabbit portions dry and season with salt and pepper. Place in a large roasting tin. Sprinkle with 2 tablespoons of the rosemary and pour over 2 tablespoons of the olive oil. Roast in the preheated oven – the loin for 7–8 minutes (it should be slightly pink) and the legs for 12–15 minutes. Remove from the oven and leave to rest for 15 minutes. Strip the meat from the bones and cut into small pieces, reserving any juices.

Meanwhile, add another 2 or 3 tablespoons of oil to the roasting tin and heat in the oven. When it's nice and hot, put in the carrots, parsnips, onions and garlic cloves, tossing to coat in the oil. Season with salt and pepper, and sprinkle with the remaining rosemary. Roast for 30 minutes until browned and soft, taking the garlic cloves out after only 15 minutes.

While the vegetables are roasting, cook the pasta according to the packet instructions. Drain and set aside.

Remove the vegetables from the roasting tin. Stir in a little stock and the reserved juices from the rabbit, and deglaze the pan on top of the stove.

Heat the remaining stock in a large saucepan, pour in the pan juices and add the rabbit, vegetables (squeeze the garlic from its skin) and cooked pasta. Simmer for 10 minutes then add the cabbage and cook for 5 minutes more until the cabbage is just tender but still brightly coloured. Check the seasoning before serving.

RABBIT SOUP WITH LEMON, GREEN PEPPERCORNS AND GRILLED POLENTA

SERVES 4

This is definitely a knife and fork soup. Supermarkets sell packs of rabbit loin cutlets which are handy for making soup. Serve with boiled potatoes and a green salad.

8 small rabbit loin cutlets, about 3 cm / 1¼ inches thick
finely grated zest of 1 large unwaxed lemon
2 tsp green peppercorns, crushed
2 tbsp olive oil
1 onion, finely chopped
4 celery stalks, thinly sliced
2 garlic cloves, finely chopped
3 large tomatoes, peeled and diced
150 g / 5½ oz Puy lentils
1.2 litres / 2 pints Chicken Stock (page 188)
2–3 thyme sprigs
salt and freshly ground black pepper
3 tbsp chopped flat-leafed parsley
Grilled Polenta (page 212)

Pat the cutlets dry and rub with the lemon zest and crushed green peppercorns. Set aside for 30 minutes.

Heat the oil in large saucepan. When it's nice and hot, fry the cutlets in a single layer (in batches if necessary) over medium–high heat for 6–8 minutes, turning until browned. Remove from the pan.

Reduce the heat and add the onion and celery to the pan. Cover and cook for about 5 minutes until softened. Add the garlic and tomato, and cook, uncovered, for a few minutes more until slightly reduced.

Return the rabbit to the pan. Add the lentils, stock and thyme sprigs, and season to taste. Bring to the boil, skimming if necessary, then simmer for 25 minutes until the rabbit and lentils are tender. Fish out the thyme stalks, check the seasoning and stir in the parsley. Serve with croûton-sized pieces of grilled polenta.

CAWL

SERVES 6

A hearty Welsh soup, traditionally served in china pudding bowls and eaten with a wooden spoon. Although filling on its own, you could also serve good farmhouse bread, Caerphilly cheese and some home-cooked ham.

450 g / 1 lb leeks, green parts included, quartered
lengthways and cut into 1 cm / $^1/_2$ inch slices
350 g / 12 oz new potatoes, unpeeled, cut into quarters
2 carrots, sliced
1 parsnip, cut into 2 cm / $^3/_4$ inch chunks
175 g / 6 oz swede, cut into 2 cm / $^3/_4$ inch chunks
1 tbsp fine oatmeal
25 g / 1 oz butter
350 g / 12 oz piece smoked bacon, derinded and
cut into 2 cm / $^3/_4$ inch cubes
2–3 thyme sprigs
1.7 litres / 3 pints Chicken Stock (page 188)
or Ham Hock Stock (page 191)
salt and freshly ground black pepper
finely chopped raw green leek, to garnish

Put the vegetables in a large bowl, sprinkle with the oatmeal and toss until coated.

Melt the butter in a large saucepan and add the bacon cubes. Fry gently over medium heat for 3–4 minutes, stirring frequently. When nicely browned, add the vegetables and thyme sprigs. Stir, then cover and sweat over low heat for 5 minutes until beginning to soften.

Pour in the stock, bring to the boil, then simmer gently, partially covered, for about 20 minutes. Use a perforated spoon to remove any scum that floats to the surface. Season to taste and garnish with a little raw leek.

Basic Stocks

In the olden days, no self-respecting cook would be without a stockpot bubbling away on the back of the stove. Nowadays, given the choice of ready-made cubes and chilled stocks available, stock-making is in danger of becoming a thing of the past. However, a fresh, home-made stock will lift an otherwise mundane soup into the realms of gastronomic excellence, and most commercially made stocks simply do not compare.

The idea of making stock may seem daunting but in reality it is very little trouble – all that's needed are patience and good quality, fresh ingredients. Stocks will keep for 4–5 days in the fridge, but it's well worth making extra to freeze for later use. This can be a life-saver on those occasions when you need to rustle up an impromptu soup for someone you want to impress.

Meat and poultry stocks require simmering for several hours, but vegetable stocks are cooked in less than an hour otherwise the flavour can become unpleasant. Vegetables for vegetable stocks should be diced quite finely (about 2 cm/¾ inches square) to increase the surface area and to encourage them to release their nourishing juices quickly.

I have included recipes for a variety of stocks to suit a wide range of soups. Many of them are interchangeable so don't worry if you don't have the one specified in the recipe. Should you find yourself without a home-made stock, Marigold Swiss vegetable bouillon powder is one of the few commercially made stocks that produces a flavourful soup without being oversalty. It is equally good in meat or vegetable soups.

THE RECIPES

VEGETABLE STOCK

MAKES 1.7–2 LITRES/3–3½ PINTS

This makes an all-purpose stock which you
can use wherever you would normally use meat
or chicken stock.

2 tbsp olive oil
2 fresh bay leaves
2 lovage sprigs
3 thyme sprigs
several large basil leaves
handful of parsley sprigs
2 onions, diced
4 celery stalks with leaves, finely diced
2 carrots, finely diced
1 small fennel bulb, finely diced
4 tomatoes, quartered
green parts from 2 leeks, finely chopped
¼ cabbage (about 115g/4 oz), finely chopped
1 small aubergine, finely diced
a few black peppercorns
1 tsp salt
2 tbsp lemon juice

Heat the oil with the herbs in a large saucepan over
medium heat. Add the vegetables and 150 ml/¼ pint of
water. Cover and cook for 10–15 minutes to soften.

Add the peppercorns and 3 litres/5¼ pints of water,
bring to the boil and simmer, partially covered, for 40
minutes. Add the salt and lemon juice.

Strain the stock through a fine-meshed sieve, pressing to
extract all the liquid.

LIGHT VEGETABLE STOCK

MAKES 2 LITRES/3$\frac{1}{2}$ PINTS

This is a delicate, pale-coloured stock to use for soups made with spring vegetables, noodles or pasta.

2 tbsp olive oil
6 fresh parsley sprigs
1 fresh bay leaf
3 thyme or tarragon sprigs
3 leeks, green parts included, quartered lengthways and chopped
3 onions, finely diced
3 celery stalks with leaves, finely diced
5 carrots, finely diced
1 small green lettuce, such as Little Gem or Sweet Romaine, sliced
3 garlic cloves, crushed
1–2 strips of lemon peel
a few peppercorns
squeeze of lemon juice

Heat the oil with the herbs in a large saucepan over medium heat. Add the vegetables and garlic and 150 ml/ $\frac{1}{4}$ pint of water. Cover and cook for 10–15 minutes to soften.

Add 1.3 litres/2$\frac{1}{4}$ pints of water along with the lemon peel and peppercorns and bring slowly to the boil. Reduce the heat and simmer, partially covered, for 40 minutes.

Strain through a fine-meshed sieve, pressing out as much of the liquid as possible. Add a squeeze of lemon juice to sharpen the flavour.

MUSHROOM STOCK

MAKES 1.4 LITRES/2½ PINTS

This stock will intensify the flavour of any soup
made with mushrooms.

25 g/1 oz dried porcini or morels
1 large onion, finely diced
1 fresh bay leaf
6 thyme sprigs
3 sage sprigs
6 parsley sprigs
250 g/9 oz chestnut mushrooms, including stalks, finely sliced
2 carrots, finely diced
1 celery stalk, finely diced
½ small fennel bulb, finely diced

Cover the dried mushrooms with boiling water and leave to
soak for 30 minutes. Strain and reserve the liquid.

Put the onion and herbs in a large saucepan with about
150 ml/¼ pint of water. Cook over a medium–high heat for
a few minutes, stirring, until the onion is soft.

Add the dried and fresh mushrooms, carrots, celery and
fennel. Cover and cook for 10 minutes, stirring occasionally.
Pour in enough water to cover by 5–7.5 cm/2–3 inches.
Pour in the mushroom soaking water, straining it through
muslin or paper towel to get rid of any grit. Bring to the
boil, then simmer over low heat, partially covered, for
45 minutes.

Strain the stock through a fine-meshed sieve, pressing to
extract all the liquid. If you want a stronger flavour, return
the stock to the pan and simmer for a little longer.

TOMATO STOCK

MAKES 2 LITRES/3½ PINTS

This fat-free stock has a warm, spicy flavour. You can use fresh tomatoes instead of canned ones, but they must have a good flavour.

1 small onion, finely diced
1 celery stalk, finely diced
1 leek, finely chopped
3 thyme sprigs
2 rosemary sprigs
6 parsley sprigs
1 fresh bay leaf
2 garlic cloves, peeled but left whole
2 kg/4½ lb Italian canned peeled tomatoes
2 strips of lemon peel
1 tsp sugar
1 tsp salt
freshly ground black pepper

Put the onion, celery, leek and herbs in a large saucepan with about 150 ml/¼ pint of water. Cook over a medium-high heat for 4–5 minutes, stirring, until the onion is soft.

Add the remaining ingredients, then cover and cook for 10 minutes, stirring occasionally. Pour in 1.5 litres/2¾ pints of water, bring to the boil, then simmer, uncovered, over low heat for 45 minutes.

Strain the stock through a fine-meshed sieve, pressing to extract all the liquid.

ROASTED TOMATO STOCK

MAKES 1.7 LITRES/3 PINTS

This is a vibrant, full–bodied stock, just right for chilled
tomato soups. It is vital that the tomatoes you use
are ripe, with a good flavour.

2 kg/4^1/$_2$ lb ripe tomatoes
2 tbsp olive oil
2 red onions, finely diced
3 celery stalks, finely diced
3 carrots, finely diced
75 g/2^3/$_4$ oz mushrooms, chopped
2 garlic cloves, finely chopped
2 thyme sprigs or ^{1}/$_2$ tsp dried thyme
6 flat-leafed parsley sprigs
2 fresh bay leaves
4 tbsp tomato purée
1 tbsp sugar
225 ml/8 fl oz dry white wine

Place the tomatoes in a clean grill pan under a preheated
very hot grill, about 10 cm/4 inches from the heat source.
Grill, turning every so often, for about 15 minutes until
the skins blacken. Tip into a food processor – including
the blackened skins and any liquid – and process until
smooth.

Meanwhile, heat the oil in a large saucepan over medium
heat. Add the onion, celery, carrots, mushrooms, garlic and
herbs. Cover and cook, stirring occasionally, until softened –
about 7 minutes. Then add the tomato purée and sugar, and
cook for another minute.

Pour in the puréed grilled tomatoes, the wine and
600 ml/1 pint of water and bring to the boil. Reduce the
heat to a gentle simmer and cook, partially covered, for

50–60 minutes until the vegetables are soft. Allow to cool then strain through a fine-meshed sieve, pressing with the back of a wooden spoon to extract as much liquid as possible.

ORIENTAL VEGETABLE STOCK

MAKES 2.8 LITRES/5 PINTS

Shiitake mushrooms and kombu (Japanese dried seaweed) give this stock a satisfying depth of flavour. Use it for clear vegetable or noodle soups.

2 pieces dried kombu weighing about 10 g/^{1}/$_4$ oz in total
3.6 litres/6 ^{1}/$_4$ pints tepid water
4 tbsp light sesame oil or sunflower oil
3 carrots, finely chopped
2 onions, finely chopped
2 leeks, white part only, finely sliced
4 celery stalks, finely diced
4 large spring onions, finely sliced
^{1}/$_2$ fennel bulb, finely chopped
115 g/4 oz shiitake mushrooms, finely chopped
6 large unpeeled garlic cloves, crushed with the flat
of a knife blade
5 cm/2 inch piece fresh ginger root, sliced
3 lemon grass stalks, halved lengthways and bruised
1 tbsp black peppercorns, cracked
3 star anise pods
2 tsp salt
small bunch fresh flat-leafed parsley
4 tbsp shoyu or tamari (Japanese soy sauce), or to taste

Cut the kombu into pieces and put in a bowl with the tepid water. Leave to soak for 1 hour.

Heat the oil in a large saucepan over medium heat. Throw in all the vegetables including the mushrooms, garlic, ginger and lemon grass. Cover and cook gently for 15 minutes until the vegetables are softened and beginning to give up their juices.

Pour in the kombu water – but not the kombu at this

stage – add the peppercorns, star anise, salt and the bunch of parsley, and bring to the boil. Then reduce to a gentle simmer, add the kombu and cook, covered, for 1 hour.

Strain in a colander, then again through a fine-meshed sieve. Pour back into the pan, check the seasoning and add shoyu to taste. If you want a more intense flavour, boil the stock a bit longer to reduce.

CHICKEN STOCK

MAKES 3 LITRES/5¼ PINTS

It's worth getting a pig's trotter for this richly flavoured, all-purpose stock. When cool, it will set to an impressive jelly.

2.25 kg/5 lb chicken, cut into pieces
1 pig's trotter (optional)
3 onions, quartered
2 leeks, split lengthways
4 carrots, halved
4 celery sticks, halved
small handful of parsley sprigs
3–4 thyme sprigs
2 fresh bay leaves
a few black peppercorns

Put the chicken and the pig's trotter, if you have one, in a large saucepan or stockpot with enough water to cover by about 5–7.5 cm/2–3 inches. Slowly bring to the boil, removing any scum. Add the remaining ingredients. Simmer over very low heat with the lid slightly askew for 3 hours.

Strain through a fine-meshed sieve into a large bowl, then strain again through a muslin-lined sieve. Leave to cool, then put in the refrigerator. When thoroughly chilled, remove the solid layer of fat from the surface.

CHINESE STOCK

MAKES 2.5 LITRES/4½ PINTS

A mixture of chicken and pork is perfect for any oriental-style soup. Trim the pork of any excess fat before cooking.

1.3 kg/3 lb chicken pieces, such as wings, thighs and drumsticks, roughly chopped
1 kg/2 lb 4 oz pork spare ribs
5 cm/2 inch piece fresh ginger root, thickly sliced
4 large, fat spring onions, green parts included, halved lengthways
3–4 tbsp rice wine or dry sherry (optional)

Put the chicken and pork in a large saucepan with 4 litres/7 pints of water. Slowly bring to the boil, skimming off any scum.

Add the ginger, spring onions, and rice wine, if using. Reduce the heat to the gentlest of simmers and cook, uncovered, for 2–3 hours.

Strain through a colander, then again through a muslin-lined sieve. Pour back into the pan and check the seasoning. Leave to cool, then chill. When thoroughly chilled, remove any solid fat from the surface.

RICH MEAT STOCK

MAKES 2.5 LITRES/4¹/₂ PINTS

This stock will lift the most mundane of soups to the realms of gastronomic euphoria. It's worth making double the quantity so you always have some in the freezer.

1.3 kg/3 lb veal bones, cut into large pieces
2 onions, quartered
1.3 kg/3 lb lean shin of beef
450 g/1 lb stewing veal
900 g/2 lb chicken wings
2 carrots, halved
2 celery stalks with leaves
2 tomatoes
55 g/2 oz fresh parsley
2 tsp salt
¹/₂ tsp freshly ground black pepper

Preheat the oven to 230°C (220°C fan oven)/gas 8. Put the veal bones and onions in a non-stick roasting tin. Roast in the preheated oven for 30 minutes, basting occasionally. Drain off the fat and transfer the bones and onions to a stockpot or large saucepan.

Trim any visible fat from the shin of beef and stewing veal, and cut the meat into large chunks. Add to the pot with the chicken. Pour in enough water to cover by 5–7.5 cm/2–3 inches. Bring to the boil, half covered, over medium heat, skimming off any scum. Add the remaining ingredients, reduce the heat and simmer very gently for 3 hours.

Strain into a bowl, then filter through a muslin-lined sieve to remove sediment and fat. Leave to cool, then chill. When thoroughly chilled, remove the solid layer of fat from the surface.

HAM HOCK STOCK

MAKES 2.5 LITRES/4½ PINTS

This is a lovely, rich, jellied stock to have in the freezer.
It makes the most mundane of soups seem special.
If using the stock right away, add the ham meat to the
soup in which the stock is used.

3 kg/6½ lb smoked or unsmoked ham hocks, cracked
1 pig's trotter
2 onions, studded with a few cloves
2 large leeks, split lengthways
3 celery stalks, halved
3 carrots, cut into chunks
1 fresh bay leaf
2 fresh thyme sprigs
6 fresh parsley sprigs
a few black peppercorns

Put the ham hocks in a large saucepan or stockpot, cover
with water, bring to the boil, then drain and discard the
water. This is to remove excess salt.

Return the bones to the pan with all the other ingredients. Cover with fresh water – about 5 litres/9 pints – and
slowly bring to the boil, removing any scum that forms on
the surface. Reduce the heat and simmer very gently for
2–3 hours.

Strain the stock, discarding the vegetables. Pull the meat
off the bone and reserve, if using for a soup. Strain the stock
again through a muslin-lined sieve. Allow to cool, then
chill. When thoroughly chilled, remove the solid layer of fat
from the surface.

LAMB STOCK

MAKES 2.5 LITRES/4½ PINTS

This will intensify the flavour of any soup made with
lamb. The veal knuckle adds richness. It is well worth
allowing time to chill the stock so that you can remove
the layer of solidified fat from the surface.

2 tbsp sunflower or groundnut oil
1.5 kg/3 lb 5 oz lamb bones from neck, shoulder or breast
1 veal knuckle, split (optional)
2 onions, studded with a few cloves
2 carrots, cut into large chunks
2 celery stalks, halved
1 leek, green part included, split lengthways
150 ml/¼ pint red wine or water
2 garlic cloves, unpeeled and left whole
2 fresh bay leaves
2 thyme sprigs
6 flat-leafed parsley sprigs
1 tbsp fresh or dried marigold petals or
2–3 nasturtium flowers (optional)
a few black peppercorns

Preheat the oven to 230°C (220°C fan oven)/gas 8. Pour
the oil into a roasting tin and put in the oven until very
hot. Spread out the lamb bones and veal knuckle, if using,
in the tin and return to the oven to brown, turning occasionally, for about 20 minutes. Transfer the bones to a large
saucepan.

Put the onions, carrots, celery and leeks in the roasting
tin, and brown for about 10 minutes, turning to prevent
burning. Then put the vegetables in the saucepan too.

Pour off excess fat from the roasting tin, then swill out
the tin with the wine or water over medium heat on top of

the stove, scraping up any sediment from the bottom of the pan. Pour the liquid into the saucepan and add enough water just to cover.

Bring to the boil slowly, skimming off the scum that forms. Add a cupful of cold water to bring any remaining scum to the surface, and skim again. Simmer very, very gently, with the lid askew, for 1 hour.

Add the garlic, herbs, flowers and peppercorns, then leave the stock at a leisurely simmer for another 2 hours.

Strain the stock. Remove any reasonably sized bits of meat from the bone to use in a soup. Discard the bones and vegetables. Strain the stock again through a muslin-lined sieve. Leave to cool, then chill. When thoroughly chilled, remove the solid layer of fat from the surface.

GAME BIRD STOCK

MAKES 2 LITRES/3½ PINTS

This is well worth making to have on hand in the freezer.
Use it for soups made with feathered game or rabbit.

2.25 kg/5 lb bones, meat and trimmings from partridge,
pheasant, pigeon
2 tbsp groundnut oil
2 onions, chopped
2 leeks, chopped
2 carrots, chopped
3 celery stalks, chopped
strip of orange peel
1 fresh bay leaf
1 thyme sprig
small handful of parsley
a few juniper berries
2–3 cloves
a few black peppercorns

Cut the game pieces into smallish chunks. Heat the oil in a
large heavy-based pan and brown the game over a fairly
brisk heat.

Add the vegetables, stir everything around, then lower
the heat, cover and leave to sweat for 10 minutes.

Pour in enough cold water to cover – about 4 litres/
7 pints – and bring slowly to the boil. Remove the grey
scum that forms.

Add the orange peel, herbs and spices. Simmer slowly,
with the lid slightly askew, for 2½ hours.

Strain, removing any bits of meat – they can be used in a
soup. Then strain again through a muslin-lined sieve. Leave
to cool, then chill. When thoroughly chilled, remove the
solid layer of fat from the surface.

RICH GAME STOCK

MAKES 2 LITRES/3½ PINTS

This will improve a meaty soup 100 per cent.
No freezer should be without it. Use the bones and
meat from furred game such as venison, wild boar
and rabbit.

*1 kg /2 lb 4 oz veal knuckle bone, sawn into
5 cm/2 inch pieces
1.3 kg/3 lb game bones, sawn into
5 cm/2 inch pieces
1.3 kg/3 lb game meat trimmings, cut into chunks
2 onions, quartered
2 large carrots, quartered
2 celery stalks, cut into chunks
3 large garlic cloves, halved
large fresh bouquet garni, including bay,
thyme, parsley, sage
1 tsp juniper berries
1 tsp black peppercorns*

Put the bones and meat in a large saucepan or stockpot with
enough water to cover by about 5 cm/2 inches. Bring
to the boil slowly, skimming off the scum. Continue to
skim, occasionally adding a glass of cold water, until no
more scum rises.

Add the remaining ingredients and skim once more as
the liquid comes to the boil. Reduce the heat to very low
and simmer for 4–5 hours with the lid slightly askew,
skimming occasionally.

Strain the stock through a muslin-lined sieve. Taste the
stock and if it is not strong enough, boil until concentrated.

Leave to cool, then refrigerate and lift off the solidified fat
before using.

FISH STOCK

MAKES ABOUT 2.8 LITRES/5 PINTS

For some inexplicable reason, satisfactory ready-made fish stock is hard to come by, so it's worth making your own to have on hand in the freezer. It can be kept for up to one month. Do not use oily fish such as mackerel, salmon or trout for fish stock – they are too strongly flavoured.

3 tbsp sunflower or grapeseed oil
2 small onions, finely sliced
white part of 1 leek, finely sliced
1 celery stalk, finely sliced
$^1/_2$ fennel bulb, finely sliced, or use 2–3 coarse outer layers
2 kg/4$^1/_2$ lb bones, heads and flesh from white fish,
such as cod, lemon sole or coley, washed and chopped
300 ml/$^1/_2$ pint white wine
6 parsley sprigs
2 lemon thyme sprigs
2 tarragon sprigs
1 lovage sprig
1 unwaxed lemon, sliced
10 black peppercorns, cracked

Heat the oil in a large saucepan, add the vegetables and soften over a low heat, covered, for about 15 minutes without letting them brown.

Add the fish, stir, then cover and cook for 5 minutes. Add the wine and bring to the boil, then boil for 5 minutes. Add 3 litres/5 pints of water and bring back to the boil, skimming off any grey scum. Add the herbs, lemon slices and peppercorns, then simmer for 20 minutes, partially covered. Do not stir the stock.

Strain into a bowl, then strain again through a muslin-lined sieve.

SHELLFISH STOCK

MAKES 1.5 LITRES/2¾ PINTS

This is invaluable for making any kind of bisque – a thick
puréed soup made with shellfish.

heads and shells from 16 large prawns, or
175 g/6 oz cheap prawns, or a mixture
juice of 1 lemon
1 onion, chopped
1 carrot, diced
1 celery stalk, diced
1 garlic clove, peeled but left whole
10 flat-leafed parsley sprigs
1 fresh bay leaf
2–3 thyme sprigs
a few black peppercorns
1 tsp salt

Rinse the prawn shells briefly under cold running water.
Lightly pound with a pestle and mortar and put in a saucepan with the lemon juice and 150 ml/¼ pint of water. Boil
rapidly for 2 minutes.

Add the remaining ingredients except the salt, and pour
in 2 litres/3½ pints of water. Bring to the boil, skim, then
simmer over medium heat for 30 minutes.

Strain through a muslin-lined sieve and season with
the salt.

Additions and Accompaniments

This chapter is full of ideas for things to put in or serve with soups. It is these embellishments which bring a soup to life, transforming it from the ordinary to the inspirational. For instance, a perfectly worthy soup of puréed pumpkin becomes star quality when sprinkled with crisp dry-fried pumpkin seeds, a smattering of brick-red chilli flakes, a swirl of cream or a slick of pumpkin seed oil. This is not simply a case of gilding the lily – judiciously chosen embellishments reflect the spirit of the soup and harmonise the flavours. They delight the eye and sharpen the appetite, and also provide the cook with an opportunity to show off his or her creative potential.

Some soups need extra accompaniments in order to qualify as a main meal or to provide balance when a nutrient is lacking. In many cases a hunk of good bread or a grating of cheese will suffice, but there are times when something more substantial is called for. Appetising salsas, crisp-fried filo parcels, fritters and pancakes, stuffed eggs, crisp vegetable sticks, spicy miniature meatballs and stuffed leaves all fit the bill.

I have given serving suggestions for accompaniments in individual recipe introductions, but these are simply ideas. There are no hard and fast rules – it's simply a question of following your tastebuds.

THE RECIPES

BLINIS

MAKES 20

These pancakes are easy to make and delicious with Central European-style soups. Top them with soured cream or smoked salmon.

85 g/3 oz buckwheat flour
85 g/3 oz plain flour
1 tsp sugar
½ tsp baking powder
½ tsp bicarbonate of soda
¼ tsp salt
350 ml/12 fl oz buttermilk
1 large egg, beaten
1 tbsp grapeseed or safflower oil, plus extra for frying

Sift all the dry ingredients into a bowl and stir to combine. Beat in the buttermilk, egg and oil.

Place a griddle or heavy-based frying pan over medium-high heat and brush with a little oil. Stir the batter, then pour 2 tablespoons of it on to the griddle or pan, spreading with the back of a metal spoon to form a 10 cm/4 inch circle. Add three or four more circles depending on the size of your griddle.

Fry for 30 seconds or until holes start to appear on the surface. Turn the blinis over and fry the other side for 30 seconds or until golden brown. Keep warm while you make the rest.

PIROSHKIS

MAKES 16

These delicious little Russian pasties are
really simple to make, especially if you use
ready-made pastry. They are good to serve
with soups that are not overly substantial.
Jellied stock keeps the fish and meat fillings
moist, but once added you will need to use the
filling right away before the stock liquefies.
Use soured cream instead of jellied stock
for the fish filling if you want to make it in
advance. Piroshkis can be baked and
frozen. Defrost and reheat at
180°C (170°C fan oven)/gas 4
for 15 minutes.

MUSHROOM FILLING
Finely chop half a small onion, 250 g/9 oz mushrooms and
1 garlic clove. Fry the onion gently in 3 tbsp olive oil until
soft. Add the mushrooms and garlic, and fry for another
7–10 minutes. Stir in 1 tsp each chopped fresh dill and
parsley, $\frac{1}{2}$ tsp lemon zest, salt and freshly ground black
pepper. Leave to cool. Stir in 1 finely chopped hard-boiled
egg. Moisten with 2–3 tbsp soured cream.

FISH FILLING
Mix 150 g/5$\frac{1}{2}$ oz boneless cooked fish (salmon, trout or
any firm white fish is fine) with 40 g/1$\frac{1}{2}$ oz cooked rice,
1 finely chopped hard-boiled egg, $\frac{1}{4}$ tsp lemon zest and
1 tsp each chopped fresh dill and parsley. Season with salt
and freshly ground black pepper. Moisten with 3 tbsp
soured cream or jellied fish stock (page 196).

MEAT FILLING

Gently fry half a finely chopped onion in 1 tbsp olive oil until soft. Add 150 g/5½ oz lean minced beef and 1 finely chopped garlic clove, and cook until the meat is no longer pink. Mix with 1 tsp each finely chopped fresh parsley and thyme, some freshly grated nutmeg, salt and freshly ground black pepper. Leave to cool. Bind with 2 tbsp beaten egg. Stir in 2–3 tbsp jellied rich meat stock (page 190) or chicken stock (page 188: made with a pig's trotter) to moisten.

TO MAKE THE PIROSHKIS

Preheat the oven to 220°C (210°C fan oven)/gas 7. Roll out thinly 250 g/9 oz shortcrust or flaky pastry. Cut into 9 cm/3½ inch diameter circles. Place a heaped teaspoon of your chosen filling in the middle. Moisten the edge with water or beaten egg. Fold over and pinch the edges together. Brush with beaten egg.

Place on a greased baking sheet and bake in the pre-heated oven for 20 minutes until golden.

LACY CHICK-PEA PANCAKES

MAKES 8

These pancakes are unusual in that they are not made with eggs. Make sure you get the oil really hot before pouring in the batter. For a spicy flavour – to go with an Indian-style soup perhaps – include the kalonji seeds, turmeric and chilli flakes. For a more neutral flavour leave the spices out. You can buy chick-pea flour and kalonji seeds in ethnic food shops and healthfood shops.

225 g/8 oz chick-pea (gram) flour
2 tsp salt
$1/_4$ tsp freshly ground black pepper
2 tsp kalonji (black onion) seeds (optional)
1 tsp ground turmeric (optional)
$1/_2$ tsp crushed chilli flakes (optional)
600 ml/1 pint water
groundnut oil for frying

Sift the flour and salt into a bowl. Mix in the black pepper and, if using, the spices. Make a well in the centre and gradually whisk in the water, drawing in all the flour from the edge, until you have a smooth batter. Cover and leave to stand for 30 minutes before using.

Heat about 1 tablespoon of the oil in a heavy-based non-stick 20–23 cm/8–9 inch frying pan. When it is almost smoking, pour in a ladleful of batter in a circular motion so that the batter is distributed right to the edges of the pan. Immediately smooth the surface with a spatula, spreading the batter evenly. Lift up the edge when just set and let any uncooked batter run underneath.

Fry over a medium-high heat for about 50 seconds each side. Transfer to a plate and keep warm in a low oven while you cook the rest.

FILO TRIANGLES

MAKES 12

Serve a plate of these spicy little parcels, warm or at room temperature, alongside a Middle Eastern-style soup. They'll disappear fast so it's worth making double the quantity.

3 tbsp olive oil
150 g/5^1/$_2$ oz lean minced beef or lamb
1 small onion, finely chopped
150 g/5 ^{1}/$_2$ oz mushrooms, finely chopped
1 garlic clove, finely chopped
^{1}/$_2$ tsp ground allspice
^{1}/$_4$ tsp ground cinnamon
finely grated zest of 1 lemon
salt and freshly ground black pepper
4 sheets filo pastry, measuring 27 × 25 cm/10 ^{3}/$_4$× 10 inch
olive oil for brushing

Heat 2 teaspoons of the oil in a small pan and brown the meat. Drain off any fat and set aside.

Heat the remaining oil and gently fry the onion until translucent. Add the mushrooms and fry for 5 minutes, then add the garlic, allspice, cinnamon, lemon zest, and salt and pepper. Fry for another minute or so. Remove from the heat and allow to cool. Mix with the meat.

Preheat the oven to 200°C (190°C fan oven)/gas 6. Cut the filo pastry into twelve long strips measuring 9 × 25 cm/ 3^1/$_2$ × 10 inches. Lightly brush one strip with oil. Place about 2 level tablespoons of the filling in the bottom left-hand corner, and fold over diagonally to form a triangle. Continue to fold until you reach the end of the strip. Repeat with the remaining strips. Bake the triangles on a non-stick baking sheet for 15–20 minutes until golden.

CHEESE TOASTS

Slightly stale French bread is fine for this. If you are trying to cut down on fat, skip brushing the bread with oil or butter, and use reduced-fat Edam or mozzarella cheese. Otherwise push the boat out and use good Cheddar, Gloucester or Parmesan. Good with any bean- or pasta-based soup or for padding out thinnish soups.

1 baguette, thickly sliced
extra-virgin sunflower oil, olive oil or melted butter
freshly grated cheese

Preheat the oven to 180°C (170°C fan oven)/gas 4. Bake the bread slices on a baking sheet for a few minutes until just crisp.

Paint one side with oil or melted butter. Sprinkle generously with coarsely grated cheese and return to oven until melted. Serve immediately.

BRUSCHETTA

Thick rounds of toasted rustic bread, rubbed with garlic
and dressed with a generous dribbling of fruity olive oil,
are perfect with hearty vegetable or bean-based soups. Add
toppings if you like.

thick slices of good crusty bread, about 7 cm/3 inches in diameter
garlic cloves, bashed
extra-virgin olive oil
sea salt flakes and freshly ground black pepper

Toast the bread in a moderate oven (180°C/170°C fan
oven/gas 4), on a griddle or, best of all, on a barbecue, until
golden brown on both sides. Rub one side of each slice
with mashed garlic. Place on a serving dish, garlic side up,
and dribble over enough olive oil to lightly soak the bread.
Sprinkle with salt and a grinding of pepper.

TOPPINGS
Roasted and mashed aubergine slices
Roasted red pepper strips
Diced fresh tomato with torn basil leaves
Grilled red onion slices with chopped fresh rosemary
Mashed fried chicken livers

CATALAN TOMATO BREAD

I first tasted this in Barcelona and have been addicted to the soft, slightly sloppy texture ever since. It is really simple to make.

3 ripe tomatoes, peeled and quartered
thick slices of rustic bread
sea salt
extra-virgin olive oil, preferably Spanish

Put the tomatoes in a blender and process to a chunky purée. Spread the purée out on a shallow dish, then press the bread into it, coating well on both sides, until the bread becomes soft and moist. Sprinkle with salt and drizzle with olive oil. Delicious!

GARLIC CROÛTONS

SERVES 4

Croûtons are great for adding flavour and crunch to a soup that needs a little livening up. They can be stored in an airtight container for about a week.

4 thick slices stale close-grained bread, crusts removed
6 tbsp olive oil or extra-virgin sunflower oil
2 garlic cloves, sliced
seasonings such as crushed chilli flakes, fresh sage, dried thyme or
oregano (optional)

Cut the bread into small cubes. Heat the oil in a large frying pan. Add the garlic and stir round for a few seconds to flavour the oil. Remove with a perforated spoon as soon as it turns golden.

Throw in the bread cubes, stirring so that they are evenly coated with the oil. Add seasonings if you like, and fry until evenly golden. Drain on crumpled paper towels.

CHILLI AND CORIANDER CORN MUFFINS

MAKES 12

These homely corn muffins are spiked with chilli and coriander – great with any Mexican-style soup.

3–4 large fresh green chillies
4 large garlic cloves, unpeeled
300 g/11 oz plain flour
150 g/5$^{1}/_{2}$ oz yellow cornmeal or polenta
1 tbsp plus 1 tsp baking powder
1$^{1}/_{2}$ tsp salt
4 eggs
8 tbsp extra-virgin sunflower oil or olive oil
225–250 ml/8–9 fl oz water
8 tbsp chopped fresh coriander

Preheat the oven to 180°C (170°C fan oven)/gas 4. Place the chillies and garlic in a small roasting tin. Roast for about 15 minutes until the chillies are beginning to blacken and blister and the garlic feels soft. Remove the skin from the garlic and the skin and seeds from the chillies. Chop the flesh roughly.

Place a non-stick 12-hole muffin or deep bun tray in the oven to warm for 5 minutes.

Sift the flour, cornmeal, baking powder and salt into a mixing bowl.

Put the chillies and garlic in a blender with the eggs, oil and water, and process until smooth. Combine this with the dry ingredients and coriander, mixing thoroughly to form a moist but not sticky dough. Add a little more water if the dough is too dry.

Spoon into the muffin tray and bake in the preheated oven for 15–20 minutes.

LATKES

MAKES 12

I can never make enough of these – they seem to disappear before we sit down to eat the soup they are intended to accompany. Potatoes vary in size and water content so you'll need to adjust the amount of flour. The mixture should be reasonably liquid. Make sure the oil is very hot before adding the potato mixture, otherwise the latkes will be greasily soggy.

2 large red-skinned potatoes, about 250 g/9 oz each
1 small onion, grated
2 eggs, lightly beaten
4–8 tbsp plain flour
1 tsp baking powder
1 tsp salt
1/4 tsp freshly ground black pepper
groundnut oil for frying
soured cream or smetana, to serve

Grate the potatoes and rinse thoroughly in several changes of water to remove all the starch. Drain and dry on a clean tea towel. Put into a bowl with the onion, eggs, 4 tablespoons of the flour, baking powder, salt and pepper. Stir to combine and add more flour if the mixture is too wet.

Pour oil into a large non-stick frying pan to a depth of 5 mm/1/4 inch, and heat over medium-high heat until very hot but not smoking.

Drop large tablespoonfuls of the mixture into the pan, pressing gently with the back of a spoon to flatten slightly. Fry for 1 1/2–2 minutes each side until golden brown and the edges are crisp. Drain on paper towels and keep warm while you cook the rest.

GRILLED POLENTA

Polenta is made from yellow cornmeal and has a satisfying mellow flavour – non-enthusiasts would say bland. Even so, small croûtons of polenta add body and brilliant colour to soups. Parmesan, basil or pine kernels provide extra flavour but are not essential. Polenta is impossible to make in small amounts, but left-overs can be kept in a sealed container in the fridge for a few days.

1 litre/1³/₄ pints cold water
1 tsp salt
225 g/8 oz polenta
85 g/3 oz coarsely grated Parmesan cheese (optional)
freshly torn basil leaves (optional)
25 g/1 oz pine kernels, dry-fried (optional)
olive oil for brushing

Put the water and salt in a large saucepan. Over medium heat, whisk in the polenta in a continuous stream, whisking constantly to stop lumps forming. Bring to the boil, stirring continuously with a wooden spoon.

Reduce the heat and simmer, stirring vigorously all the time (or for as long as you can bear), until the mixture starts to pull away from the sides of the pan – about 15 minutes. Stir in the cheese, basil and/or pine kernels at this point, if you're including them.

Pour the mixture into a 30 × 23 cm/12 × 9 inch baking tin or shallow dish, levelling the surface with a wet knife or damp hands. It should form a layer about 1cm/¹/₂ inch thick. Leave to cool at room temperature until firm.

Cut into your preferred shape and size – cubes, diamonds or whatever. Brush with oil and toast under the grill or in a very hot oven until crisp and beginning to brown around the edges.

OMELETTE CHUNKS

MAKES ENOUGH FOR 4–6 SERVINGS OF SOUP

Thick chunks of omelette add substance and protein to clear vegetable soups. Leave out the Parmesan and herbs if serving with an oriental soup, and instead add a teaspoonful of finely chopped fresh ginger and some chopped spring onion.

3 eggs
salt and freshly ground black pepper
2 tbsp chopped fresh herbs such as
sorrel, chives or flat-leafed parsley (optional)
1 tbsp freshly grated Parmesan cheese (optional)
15 g/$^1/_2$ oz butter

Beat the eggs with the seasonings, herbs and Parmesan, if using. Heat the butter in a 20 cm/8 inch non-stick frying pan until foaming. Pour in the beaten egg mixture and cook for a few minutes until set, tilting the pan and lifting the edge to allow uncooked egg to run underneath.

Slide on to a board and cut into chunks or thin strips.

STUFFED EGGS

SERVES 6

Starting the eggs off in cold water produces perfectly textured yolks and also prevents the shells from cracking. The timing is important – cook the eggs any longer and you will have dry, powdery yolks that won't cling together to make a moist stuffing.

7 large eggs, preferably organic free-range

CUMIN AND CORIANDER STUFFING
¼ tsp salt
1 tsp ground cumin
1 tbsp finely chopped fresh coriander
2 tsp lemon juice
2 tbsp plain yogurt

Put the eggs in a saucepan with cold water to cover. Bring to the boil, then boil for exactly 5 minutes. Drain under cold running water and leave to cool.

Remove the shells and slice the eggs in half lengthways. Put the yolks in a bowl and mash well with a fork. Add the salt, cumin, coriander, lemon juice and yogurt. Either eat the untidiest pair of whites, or chop them very finely and add to the mixture.

Spoon the filling into the cavities of twelve of the neatest egg whites, piling it up generously.

SUN–DRIED TOMATO AND TABASCO STUFFING
1 tbsp sun-dried tomato purée, ¼ tsp salt, 1 tsp Tabasco sauce, 1 tbsp finely chopped fresh flat-leafed parsley, 1 tbsp plain yogurt, freshly ground black pepper. Make as described above.

LEMON AND CHIVE STUFFING

1 tbsp lemon juice, 2 tbsp plain yogurt, 2 tbsp chopped fresh chives, $\frac{1}{4}$ tsp salt, freshly ground black pepper. Make as described above.

DILL AND CAPER STUFFING

2 tbsp mayonnaise, 1 tbsp Dijon mustard, 1 tbsp chopped fresh dill or 1 tsp dill seeds, 2 tsp drained, rinsed and chopped capers, freshly ground black pepper. Make as described above.

STUFFED LEAVES

MAKES 12

Stuffed leaves provide soups with surprise packets of flavour. Serve warm, either in the soup or on the side.

12 medium-sized cabbage leaves or crisp lettuce leaves

MUSHROOM, DILL AND LEMON STUFFING
1 tbsp olive oil
225 g/8 oz mushrooms, finely diced
1 garlic clove, finely chopped
finely grated zest of 1 large lemon
3 tbsp chopped fresh dill
salt and freshly ground black pepper

Plunge the leaves into a large pan of boiling water for a few seconds (cabbage leaves for 30 seconds, lettuce leaves for 10) until wilted. Drain under cold running water. Using a small, sharp knife, shave away any thick parts of stalk. Spread out to dry on paper towels.

Heat the oil in a frying pan. Add the mushrooms and fry over medium-high heat for about 5 minutes until most of the liquid has evaporated. Add the garlic, lemon zest, dill and seasonings, and cook for another minute. Allow the mixture to cool a little, then divide between the leaves, placing it on the stalk end. Fold over the bottom, then the sides of each leaf, and roll up to make a neat parcel.

Place the leaves seam-side down in a single layer in a steamer basket (cook in batches if necessary) over boiling water. Cover and steam for 8 minutes if using cabbage leaves and 4–5 minutes if using lettuce leaves.

TOMATO, MINT AND RICE STUFFING
Mix together the following ingredients until thoroughly blended: 60 g/2¼ oz cooked white or brown long-grain rice; 2 finely diced tomatoes; 2 finely chopped spring onions; 4 tbsp chopped fresh mint; ¼ tsp ground cinnamon; ¼ tsp freshly ground black pepper; salt. Divide between the leaves and cook as above.

LAMB AND RICE STUFFING
Mix together the following ingredients until thoroughly blended: 115 g/4 oz minced lamb; 40 g/1½ oz cooked white or brown long-grain rice; 1 tbsp grated onion; 1 tbsp pine nuts (optional), dry-fried; 1 tbsp chopped fresh flat-leafed parsley; ¼ tsp ground cinnamon or allspice; salt and freshly ground black pepper. Divide between the leaves and cook as above.

SPICED NUT STUFFING
Put the following ingredients into a blender and grind to a rough paste: 175 g/6 oz chopped unsalted cashews or peanuts; 4 tbsp chopped fresh coriander; 2 tbsp cumin seeds, dry-fried and ground; 2.5 cm/1 inch piece fresh ginger root, very finely chopped; 1 tbsp lemon juice; ½ tsp each chilli powder and ground turmeric; 1 tsp each salt and sugar; 3 tbsp groundnut oil. Divide between the leaves and cook as above.

SPICED RED PEPPER AND COUSCOUS STUFFING
Heat 1 tbsp groundnut oil in a saucepan over medium heat. Add 1 fresh green chilli, deseeded and finely chopped; 2 cm/¾ inch piece fresh ginger root, very finely chopped and ½ tsp cumin seeds, and fry for a few seconds. Then add half a very finely chopped red pepper, and stir-fry until soft. Stir in 40 g/1½ oz couscous and 6 tbsp stock or water, and cook for 1 minute. Remove from the heat and stir in 2 tbsp chopped fresh coriander

or flat-leafed parsley; 1 tsp lemon juice; $\frac{1}{4}$ tsp salt; some freshly ground black pepper. Cover and set aside for 5 minutes. Fluff with a fork. Divide between the leaves and cook as above.

MATZO BALLS

MAKES 15–20 BALLS

Matzo balls and chicken soup must be one of the most restoring soups ever. You can buy matzo meal from Jewish delicatessens, otherwise grind matzo crackers (widely available in supermarkets) to a coarse powder in a food processor. If you like, cook the balls in water, remove with a perforated spoon and refrigerate until ready to add to soup. Otherwise cook them directly in the soup.

1 egg and 1 egg yolk
4–6 tbsp Chicken Stock (page 188)
2 tbsp grapeseed or sunflower oil
115 g/4 oz matzo meal or finely ground matzo crackers
1 tbsp chopped fresh parsley
2 tbsp chopped fresh dill or chives
¹/₂ tsp salt
freshly ground black pepper

Beat the egg and extra yolk with the stock and oil. Stir in the matzo meal, herbs and seasoning. Add more stock if the mixture seems dry. Chill for 30 minutes. Form into 2.5 cm/1 inch balls – don't press the mixture together too much or you will end up with leaden cannon balls instead of soft pillows.

Drop into boiling salted water, or directly into soup, and simmer very gently, covered, for 30 minutes.

DUMPLINGS

Dumplings are standard soup fodder the world over. You can cook them in water and reheat them in the soup later on – this seems to give a lighter result; otherwise drop them directly into the soup to cook. The cooking liquid should simmer gently – if you allow it to boil, your dumplings are in danger of disintegrating.

LEMON PEPPER DUMPLINGS
115 g/4 oz plain flour
1 tsp baking powder
$^1/_2$ tsp salt
1 tsp freshly ground black pepper
15 g/$^1/_2$ oz butter or sunflower margarine
finely grated zest of 1 lemon
1 egg
2–3 tbsp milk

Sift the flour, baking powder and salt together. Add the pepper. Rub in the butter or margarine until the mixture looks like coarse crumbs. Add the lemon zest. Beat the egg and milk and stir into the flour mixture to form a soft dough. With floured hands, form the mixture into 4 cm/1$^1/_2$ inch balls. Cook for about 15 minutes.

HERB DUMPLINGS
Follow the recipe for Lemon Pepper Dumplings, leaving out the pepper and lemon zest and adding instead 2 tbsp finely chopped fresh parsley and 2 tbsp finely chopped fresh basil, dill or other herb of your choice.

CHEESE DUMPLINGS
Follow the recipe for Lemon Pepper Dumplings, leaving out the pepper and lemon zest and adding 50 g/1$^3/_4$ oz of grated cheese instead.

BACON AND ONION DUMPLINGS
15 g/¹/₂ oz butter or sunflower margarine
1 tbsp finely chopped onion
1 garlic clove, finely chopped
1 tbsp fresh thyme leaves
115 g/4 oz unsmoked lean bacon, derinded and
very finely chopped
85 g/3 oz fresh breadcrumbs
¹/₂ tsp salt
freshly ground black pepper
2 tbsp plain flour
1–2 tbsp stock

Melt the butter in a small pan and gently fry the onion, garlic and thyme for 1 minute. Mix with the bacon, breadcrumbs, salt, pepper and flour – you can do this in a blender if you like. Mix in enough stock to enable the mixture to stick together. Form into 2.5 cm/1 inch balls. Cook for 10 minutes.

ORIENTAL FISH DUMPLINGS
250 g/9 oz fish fillets (white fish, trout or
salmon) or peeled prawns
4 tbsp finely chopped spring onion tops or garlic chives
2 cm/³/₄ inch piece fresh ginger root, finely chopped
¹/₂ tsp salt
freshly ground black pepper
2 egg whites, lightly beaten
3–4 tbsp plain flour

Grind the fish or prawns to a paste in a blender, or with a pestle and mortar. Transfer to a bowl and mix in the spring onions, ginger, salt and pepper. Stir in the egg whites. Add enough flour to make a soft dough. Form into 2 cm/³/₄ inch balls. Cook for 5 minutes.

THREE MEAT BALLS

EACH TYPE MAKES ABOUT
24 WALNUT-SIZED BALLS

These add body and protein to soups, and are useful if you are catering simultaneously for vegetarians and meat-eaters — make a vegetarian soup and add meatballs to the carnivores' serving. Meatballs can be made in advance and either stored in the fridge or frozen.

ITALIAN BEEF BALLS
350 g/12 oz lean finely minced beef
4 tbsp grated onion
1 garlic clove, crushed or very finely chopped
$1^1/_2$ tbsp tomato purée
$1^1/_2$ tbsp freshly grated Parmesan cheese
2 tbsp finely chopped flat-leafed parsley
$^1/_2$ tsp dried oregano
1 small egg, beaten
salt and freshly ground black pepper

LEMON AND MINT TURKEY BALLS
350 g/12 oz minced turkey
4 tbsp grated onion
1 garlic clove, crushed or very finely chopped
finely grated rind and juice of $^1/_2$ lemon
2 tbsp finely chopped fresh mint
1 small egg, beaten
8 tbsp breadcrumbs
salt and freshly ground black pepper

LEBANESE LAMB BALLS

350 g/12 oz extra lean finely minced lamb
4 tbsp grated onion
1 garlic clove, crushed or very finely chopped
1/2 tsp ground cumin
1/4 tsp ground cinnamon
1/4 tsp ground allspice
2 tbsp finely chopped fresh flat-leafed parsley
salt and freshly ground black pepper

Mix the ingredients in a blender until smooth. Form into 24 walnut-sized balls. Place on a plate and chill for 30 minutes. Heat 2–3 tablespoons of groundnut oil in a non-stick frying pan over medium heat. Fry the balls for 5–8 minutes, turning occasionally, until evenly browned and cooked through. Drain on paper towels.

THREE RED SAUCES

These are invaluable for adding zest and colour, and are
guaranteed to liven up any soup.

PEBRE
No Chilean table would be complete without a bowl of this
fiery brew. Use it to spread on crusty bread to eat with your
soup, or even swirl it into the soup. Proportions of
ingredients vary from household to household, so use more
or less of anything as you think fit.

In a bowl, combine 2 chopped deseeded tomatoes, 1
chopped small yellow onion, 2 finely chopped garlic cloves,
1 finely chopped small hot red fresh chilli, and 1 tbsp each
chopped fresh coriander and flat-leafed parsley. Add 2 tbsp
extra-virgin olive oil and 2 tsp red wine vinegar, and season
with salt and freshly ground black pepper. Cover and set
aside for about an hour so the flavours can blend. Makes
300 ml/$\frac{1}{2}$ pint.

ROUILLE
This pungent sauce from Provence is traditionally served
with hearty fish soups.

Dissolve a good pinch of saffron threads in 2–3 tbsp hot
water or soup. Put 40 g/1$\frac{1}{2}$ oz fresh breadcrumbs in a bowl
and mash with the saffron solution. Add a bit more liquid if
necessary to form a slightly sloppy paste.

Roast 1–2 fresh fat red chillies in a hot oven or under the
grill until the skin blackens and blisters. When cool enough
to handle, remove the seeds and skin. Chop the flesh and
pound to a thick paste, using a pestle and mortar, with 4
cloves of garlic and a large pinch of sea salt flakes. Mix with
1 egg yolk and the saffron breadcrumbs. Gradually trickle in
4–6 tbsp good olive oil, beating until you have a
mayonnaise-like sauce. Makes 200 ml/7 fl oz.

ROASTED PEPPER CREAM

Use yellow or red peppers to provide a contrasting colour to the soup in which you are going to swirl it. The cream will keep in a screw-top jar in the fridge for about a week.

Roast 1 pepper as above (and half a small fresh red chilli if you like heat). When cool enough to handle, remove the seeds and skin. Purée until smooth with 3 tbsp wholemilk organic yogurt or whipping cream, and salt and pepper to taste. Makes 120 ml/4 fl oz.

For a spicier version, add to the purée 1½ tbsp sun-dried tomato paste, 1 tbsp olive oil, ½ tsp crushed dry-fried coriander seeds, a thumbnail-sized piece of finely chopped fresh ginger root and ½ tsp finely grated lemon zest.

THREE GREEN SAUCES

These brilliant green piquant sauces add sharpness and
colour to all kinds of soups.

SALSA VERDE
Good with meat or fish soup. If made in advance, leave out
the vinegar or lemon juice and add it just before serving.
The sauce will keep in a screw-top jar in the fridge for up to
a week. Allow to come to room temperature and mix well
before using.

3 tbsp chopped fresh flat-leafed parsley
2 tbsp chopped mixed herbs such as thyme, basil, rocket, chervil,
tarragon, savory, lovage
3 tbsp capers, rinsed and chopped
1 garlic clove, finely chopped
1 1/2 tsp Dijon mustard
salt and freshly ground black pepper
1–3 tsp red wine vinegar or 2 tbsp lemon juice
150 ml/ 1/4 pint extra-virgin olive oil

Put all the ingredients except the oil in a food processor or
blender. Add 4 tablespoons of the oil and whizz to a paste.
With the motor still running, gradually trickle in the rest
of the oil until the sauce forms a uniform consistency.
Makes 200 ml/7 fl oz.

PESTO
Good with pasta or bean soups. Put 50 g/1 3/4 oz roughly
torn basil leaves in a food processor or blender with 2–4
crushed garlic cloves and 3 tbsp pine kernels and purée to
a smooth paste. Scrape the mixture into a bowl and stir in
3 tbsp freshly grated Parmesan or Pecorino Sardo cheese.
Makes about 100 ml/3 1/2 fl oz.

AVOCADO AND CHILLI SAUCE

Good with tomato or bean soups. Put 1 large diced avocado in a food processor or blender with 1 tbsp juice from a jar of pickled chillies. Add 1 tbsp chopped fresh coriander, 1 chopped spring onion, 1 chopped and deseeded green chilli, 1 crushed garlic clove, salt and about 4 tbsp water. Purée until thick and smooth. Makes 300 ml/½ pint.

THREE SALSAS

SERVE 4–6

Salsas add zest and colour to any smooth, vegetable or pulse-based soup. Use within 3–4 hours otherwise the salsa loses its vibrancy. The first two salsas add body to summery Mexican-style vegetable soups – serve alongside the soup or dunk a spoonful on top. Chick-Pea and Feta Salsa is good to serve with tomato-based or Mediterranean-style soups.

GRILLED CORN, AVOCADO AND TOMATO SALSA
1 sweetcorn ear, without husks
$^1/_2$ large avocado, finely diced
2 tomatoes, deseeded and finely diced
2 tbsp finely diced red onion
1 small fresh chilli, deseeded and very finely diced
2 tbsp lime juice
sea salt flakes

Put the corn on a baking sheet under a very hot grill. Grill for 10–12 minutes, turning occasionally. Allow to cool, then scrape the kernels from the cobs with a small sharp knife.

Put the kernels in a bowl with the remaining ingredients.

BLACK BEAN SALSA
115 g/4 oz black beans, soaked overnight, or
225 g /8 oz drained canned beans
3 tbsp finely diced red onion
$^1/_2$ fresh or roasted red pepper, finely diced
$^1/_2$ fresh green or red chilli, deseeded and very finely diced
juice of 1 lime
2 tbsp chopped fresh coriander
sea salt flakes, to taste

Drain the soaked beans and put in a saucepan with plenty of fresh water to cover. Bring to the boil and boil rapidly for 15 minutes. Reduce the heat to a brisk simmer and continue to cook for another 15–30 minutes until the beans are tender but not breaking up. Drain and leave to cool. If using canned beans, rinse them well and set aside.

Mix with the remaining ingredients and leave to stand at room temperature for about 30 minutes to let the flavours develop.

CHICK–PEA AND FETA SALSA

115 g/4 oz chick-peas, soaked overnight, or
225 g/8 oz drained canned chick-peas
3 tbsp finely chopped spring onion, green parts included
3 tomatoes, peeled, deseeded and very finely diced
3 tbsp chopped fresh flat-leafed parsley
2 tbsp lemon juice
sea salt flakes and freshly ground black pepper
50 g/1³⁄₄ oz feta cheese, crumbled

Drain the soaked chick-peas and put in a saucepan with plenty of fresh water to cover. ring to the boil and boil rapidly for 15 minutes. Reduce the heat to a brisk simmer and continue to cook for about another 25–35 minutes until tender. Drain and leave to cool. If using canned chick-peas, rinse them well and set aside.

Mix with the onion, tomatoes, parsley, lemon juice and seasoning. Scatter the cheese over the top.

AÏOLI

MAKES ABOUT 150 ML/¼ PINT

Delicious with toasted French bread as an accompaniment
to Mediterranean–style fish or vegetable soups. Make sure
all the ingredients are at room temperature.

4–6 garlic cloves
pinch of sea salt flakes
1 egg yolk
1½ tsp lemon juice
150 ml/¼ pint olive oil
freshly ground black pepper

Pound the garlic and salt to a smooth paste with a pestle and
mortar. Transfer to a small bowl. Add the egg yolk and ½
teaspoon of lemon juice, and whisk until thick – this will
take about 1 minute. Trickle in the oil, drop by drop,
whisking constantly. Once the mixture has become very
thick, you can add the oil in a very thin stream, still
whisking constantly. Stir in the remaining lemon juice and
add pepper and more salt if necessary.

CORIANDER CREAM

MAKES 150 ML/¼ PINT

Cooling and astringent, this cream is good in richly flavoured meat or fish soups as well as summery vegetable soups.

50 g/1³/4 oz fresh coriander, trimmed and roughly chopped
2 spring onions, chopped
1 small garlic clove, chopped
juice of 1 lime
½ tsp of cumin seeds, dry-fried
4 tbsp of Greek yogurt
3 tbsp of double cream
salt and freshly ground black pepper

In a blender, purée the fresh coriander, spring onions, garlic, lime juice and cumin seeds. You will need to run the machine for 2–3 minutes and keep scraping down the sides of the goblet. Pour the mixture into a bowl and stir in the Greek yogurt and double cream. Season to taste with salt and pepper.

LIME-THYME CREAM

MAKES 150 ML/¼ PINT

This is good with poultry or seafood soups.

125 ml/4 fl oz crème fraîche
juice and finely grated zest of ½ lime
2 tsp finely chopped fresh thyme
salt and freshly ground black pepper

Combine all the ingredients in a small bowl. Leave to stand for at least 30 minutes to allow the flavours to develop.

SAFFRON CREAM

MAKES 200 ML/7 FL OZ

This adds colour and a musky flavour. It is particularly
good with fish soups.

¹/₄ tsp saffron threads
1 tbsp hot water
150 ml/¹/₄ pint double cream
100 ml/3¹/₂ fl oz fish, vegetable or chicken stock
salt and freshly ground black pepper

Grind the saffron threads to a rough powder with a pestle
and mortar. Add the hot water and leave to infuse for about
5 minutes.

Pour the double cream into a small saucepan with your
chosen stock (depending on the soup the cream is intended
to garnish). Stir in the saffron solution. Bring to the boil
then simmer for about 5 minutes, stirring, until thickened.
Season with salt and freshly ground black pepper.

ROASTED GARLIC CREAM

MAKES ABOUT 150 ML/¼ PINT

Garlic takes on a sweetish subtle flavour in this fragrant cream. Use it in fish soups or Mexican-style soups.

1 large head of garlic
225 ml/8 fl oz double cream
sliver of lemon peel
salt and freshly ground black pepper
lemon juice

Preheat the oven to 200°C (190°C fan oven)/gas 6. Separate the garlic cloves, removing as much of the papery skin as possible but leaving a thin layer intact. Put in a small tin and roast in the preheated oven for 7–10 minutes until soft.

When cool enough to handle, remove the peel and put the cloves in a small saucepan with the cream and the lemon peel. Bring to the boil, then simmer gently for 2–3 minutes until thickened.

Push the sauce through a fine-meshed sieve, pressing with the back of a wooden spoon.

Reheat gently and season lightly with salt and pepper and perhaps the minutest dash of lemon juice.

ROASTED CHILLI CREAM
Replace the garlic with 1–3 fleshy, green chillies, – depending on your level of tolerance – and leave out the lemon peel and juice. Roast the chillies in a hot oven until the skin blisters and blackens, but do not over-roast or the flesh may disintegrate. When cool enough to handle, remove the skin and seeds, and roughly chop the flesh before adding to the cream. Simmer, sieve and season as for garlic cream.

SIZZLED HERBS

SERVES 4

Robust herbs sizzled until crisp in a flavoursome oil add colour and texture to smooth, thick soups. The herbs will crisp as they cool. The oil adds a silky richness.

5 tbsp extra-virgin sunflower oil or olive oil
4 tbsp chopped fresh sage, parsley or marjoram

Heat the oil in a small frying pan until very hot. Throw in the herbs and sizzle for a few seconds until crisp. Swirl herbs and a slick of oil on top of the soup, and serve at once.

Glossary of Ingredients

Most of the ingredients for the soups in this book can be found in large supermarkets, good healthfood shops or ethnic food shops. Some ingredients may be unfamiliar but I would encourage you to seek them out so that you can expand your culinary experience and create more interesting, flavourful soups. In most cases, however, I have suggested an alternative if an unusual ingredient is likely to prove elusive.

CHEESE

Hard cheeses such as Parmesan, Wensleydale and Cheddar add richness and body to soups. They are also a valuable source of protein and calcium, and can transform an ordinary soup into a satisfying and nutritionally balanced meal. Cheese can be finely grated to sprinkle over a soup, or diced into small cubes and placed in the bottom of serving bowls, or grilled on rounds of crusty bread until bubbling and then floated raft-like over a soup.

Hard cheeses are undeniably high in fat, around 30 per cent, but you need use only a small amount. Feta cheese contains less fat – around 20 per cent – and adds a lovely salty tangy flavour when crumbled into a soup.

CHILLIES

Supermarkets are at last beginning to stock named types of chillies, ranging from the mildly hot Anaheim to those with melt-down capacity such as the Habanero and Scotch Bonnet. If you are unfamiliar with a particular type of chilli, it's best to taste a tiny piece before it goes into the soup. Then, depending on your level of heat tolerance, add the smaller or larger quantity of chilli specified in the recipe. In most cases the flavour mellows during the soup-making process and ends up as a pleasing background warmth.

A word of warning to the uninitiated: after preparing chillies always thoroughly scrub utensils and, more importantly, your hands. Do not touch your eyes, mouth or other tender places until after you have done so – unless you want to experience an uncomfortable burning glow for hours to come.

Dried whole chillies are somewhat different to the fresh kind. They come in fascinating shapes, sizes and colours, with rich earthy flavours similar in complexity to those of fine wines, and some of them are not at all hot. The Cool Chile Company sells a very good range which you will find in good healthfood stores and specialist food shops.

You can also buy dried chilli flakes which are useful for sprinkling over soups to add colour and just a touch of heat.

COCONUT MILK

Using coconut milk to replace some of the stock gives a delicious Asian flavour to soups, especially when combined with zesty seasonings such as fresh coriander, lime and lemon grass. I particularly like coconut milk in soups with chicken or dark leafy greens. Canned coconut milk is becoming easier to find in supermarkets. It is also available as a powder or as a compressed block of cream, both of which can be reconstituted with hot water.

CREAM

A dollop of cream swirled into a soup not only looks attractive but adds richness and velvety texture. However, a light touch is essential since too much cream is not only cloying but may also muddy the individual flavours of the soup.

Thick and delicious, crème fraîche is particularly good. It has a mild tangy flavour, but it is 40 per cent fat. If this is a cause for concern, use a reduced-fat version, or try soured cream (20 per cent fat) which tastes slightly sharper, or smetana (10 per cent fat) made from single cream, skimmed milk and a souring agent.

FATS AND OILS

I prefer to use a good quality vegetable oil rather than butter or margarine for preliminary frying of vegetables. Grapeseed, sunflower and safflower oils are all flavourless and clean-tasting and can be used interchangeably. Groundnut oil is good for frying at a high temperature – when sizzling herbs for instance – as it has a high smoke point and does not burn easily. For a little more flavour use a light olive oil, or the delicious extra-virgin sunflower oil which is making a welcome appearance in the supermarkets. It's good in Asian-style soups where olive oil would be inappropriate.

A slick of a more strongly flavoured oil can be swirled over soup as a garnish. Good ones to try are rich, amber pumpkin seed oil, toasted sesame oil, any of the nut oils – walnut, pistachio, pine seed – and of course good fruity extra-virgin olive oil.

GRAINS AND PULSES

Grains and pulses make some of the best-tasting soups. There is an enormous variety available but surprisingly many of them do not play a regular part in the Western diet. Instead of rice and bulgar wheat, try couscous, quinoa and farro (spelt) – one of the most ancient of grains. Look for the old-fashioned heritage pulses, currently enjoying a revival amongst connoisseurs. Try richly marbled purple and cream appaloosa beans, pretty pink and brown borlotti beans or mysterious earthy black beans.

You will find many of these in good healthfood shops, and supermarkets are beginning to stock a wider range too. Middle-Eastern food shops are another rich source, and there are also specialist mail-order companies.

Soaking and cooking times for pulses will vary, depending on age and type. There are some superb Spanish haricot and black beans on the market which need hardly any soaking and cook in no time at all. Other types need overnight soaking and may take up to an hour of brisk simmering, especially if they are old. It's best to buy small quantities from a supplier with a fast turnover and use them as you need them.

HARISSA SAUCE

This is a startlingly hot purée of red peppers, chillies, garlic and a multitude of spices. It is used as a condiment in North Africa and is an essential accompaniment to couscous. The addition of a small blob can bring a pulse- or grain-based soup to life. Harissa is sold in tubes or small cans or jars which you'll find in large supermarkets or shops selling Middle-Eastern food.

HERBS

Herbs add distinctive but subtle flavours to soups. Sometimes a mixture of herbs, known as a bouquet garni, is used. A bouquet garni usually includes a few parsley and thyme sprigs, a bay leaf and maybe a small piece of celery or leek. The herbs are tied in a bunch so that they can be easily removed from the soup before serving.

Single herbs appropriate to a particular type of soup are

also good. Dill and lovage, for example, are perfect for Eastern European-style soups; chopped fennel fronds, sage or rosemary are delicious with bean-based soups; and fresh coriander is a must for spicy Asian and Mexican soups. A scattering of chives, mint or parsley, preferably the flat-leafed kind, will uplift the most mundane of soups.

Epazote, a Mexican herb little known in Europe, is lovely in bean soups – it is claimed to counteract bean-induced flatulence. It has a somewhat obnoxious smell, similar to kerosene, which disappears once cooked. I have never seen epazote in the shops but you can get the seeds from specialist seed companies, and it is very easy to grow. If you don't have any, use oregano or thyme instead.

Pungent herbs such as sage, lovage, thyme and rosemary can be added early on while the soup is cooking. Coriander, parsley and chives, however, are best sprinkled over soup just before serving. They seem to lose their flavour if added earlier.

Another way with herbs is to sizzle pungent and robust ones – sage or parsley sprigs, for example – in very hot oil, then swirl the whole lot into the soup (see page 235). The effect is deliciously hot, aromatic and crisp.

For most soups, fresh herbs are preferable to dried, though thyme and marjoram are sufficiently robust to be used dried. Both benefit from dry-frying to bring out their flavour. Just put the required amount of dried herb in a small heavy-based pan without any oil. Heat gently, stirring, for a few seconds until you can smell the aroma. Be careful not to let it burn.

SALT AND PEPPER

I prefer to use coarse sea salt flakes as a seasoning. You do not need so much as ordinary salt, and a few flakes sprinkled over a soup at the last minute provides crunchy little bursts of flavour. Always use freshly ground pepper, preferably

Tellichery peppercorns, if you can find them. Compared with other varieties, these taste amazingly fresh and peppery. Whatever type of pepper you use, the flavour and appearance of your soup will be improved if peppercorns are coarsely ground or cracked with a pestle and mortar, rather than ground to a dust.

SEEDS

Pumpkin, sunflower or sesame seeds not only look beautiful sprinkled over soup, they also add texture as well as valuable fibre, vitamins and minerals. Seeds can also be ground to a coarse powder and stirred into soups as a thickener – far less cloying than traditional thickeners such as flour or egg yolk. As with dried herbs, seeds benefit from dry-frying to bring out the flavour.

SOY SAUCE

I prefer to use traditionally made Japanese soy sauce, preferably organic, such as shoyu or tamari (wheat-free). These have a warm, mellow flavour and do not seem to be as salty as Chinese soy sauce. You can buy them in healthfood shops and large supermarkets.

SPICES

Most spices benefit from dry-frying to intensify their flavour. Cumin and coriander seeds are delicious dry-fried and crushed, then mixed with nuts or seeds to use as a thickener or garnish. Spices can also be sizzled in oil and poured over soup as a potent flavouring – a process known as tempering in Indian cookery. Try a mixture of cardamom, mustard seeds, cumin seeds and ground turmeric.

Spices quickly lose their potency if exposed to light, heat or air, so buy them in small quantities and store in an airtight container in a cool, dark cupboard.

Index

aïoli, 230; roasted tomato, red pepper and red onion soup with aïoli and sizzled sage, 16

almonds: Catalan fish soup with garlic and almonds, 122; mushroom and red pepper soup with almond and garlic picada, 34; spicy lamb and yogurt soup, 164

appaloosa beans, 239; dried and fresh bean soup with chilli and rice, 54; pork, beans and greens soup with coriander and lime, 152

asafoetida: dhal soup with carrots and cashew nuts, 74; mung bean and leafy green soup, 78

asparagus: asparagus gazpacho, 20; spring minestrone, 88

aubergines: bruschetta, 207; chick-pea and grilled aubergine soup with yogurt and mint, 56; couscous soup with roasted vegetables, 68; roasted aubergine, red pepper and chilli soup, 10; roasted aubergine and peanut soup, 8; vegetable stock, 180

avocados: avocado, green pepper and coriander soup, 6; avocado and chilli sauce, 227; chilled tomato, cucumber and pitta bread soup, 18; grilled corn, avocado and tomato salsa, 228

bacon: bacon and onion dumplings, 221; baked potato and cheese soup, 31; borlotti bean and rice soup, 48; butternut squash, tomato and black bean soup, 36; cawl, 176; farro soup, 58; pheasant, pancetta and red cabbage soup, 144; Scotch broth, 160; split-pea and bacon soup, 72; wheat grain, leek and carrot soup, 80; wild rice, mushroom and hazelnut soup, 60; winter minestrone, 90

baked potato and cheese soup, 31

barley: cockaleekie, 126; Scotch broth, 160

basil: pesto, 226; spring minestrone, 88; Thai beef and noodle soup, 98; Tuscan tomato and bread soup, 3

bass: Catalan fish soup with garlic and almonds, 122

bean sprouts: Thai beef and noodle soup, 98

beans: black and white bean soup with red pepper and chorizo, 52; dried and fresh bean soup with chilli and rice, 54; mixed bean and grain soup with green beans, tomatoes and sweetcorn, 62; *see also* black beans, borlotti beans, broad

spring onion, 92; spring
vegetable soup with leafy greens,
26
wheat grain, leek and carrot soup,
80
white bean and fennel soup with
fennel and parsley gremolata,
50
wild boar: game and lentil soup,
166; rich game stock, 195
wild rice, mushroom and hazelnut
soup, 60
winter: minestrone, 90; vegetable
soup with dumplings, 36

yams: callaloo with prawns, 114
yogurt: chick-pea and grilled
aubergine soup with yogurt
and mint, 56; coriander cream,
231; Lebanese lentil and
spinach soup, 64; spicy lamb
and yogurt soup, 164